Confronting
CHRIST

by ELTON TRUEBLOOD

Professor of Philosophy, Earlham College

WORD BOOKS, Publisher
Waco, Texas

Acknowledgment

It is a pleasure to express my gratitude to my former teacher, Dr. William E. Berry, now Emeritus Professor of Greek in Earlham College. I have been immeasurably aided in the preparation of the present work by the careful and complete literal translation of the Gospel of Mark which he put at my disposal. Dr. Berry's willingness to share with me in this enterprise is only the most recent of many evidences of his friendship since the beginning of my freshman year in Penn College.

E. T.

Earlham College
January, 1960

CONFRONTING CHRIST

Copyright © 1960 by David Elton Trueblood

E-N

Library of Congress catalog card number: 60-7955

Contents

Introduction

There has appeared, in our generation, an encouraging increase in the determination of Christian people to undertake the discipline of daily devotional reading. Difficulties appear, however, in translating desire into actual experience. Many, who are wholly sincere in the recognition of need and the decision to do something to meet it, do not know where to turn. They want to read the Bible, but they do not know how or where to begin. They are sure they need help, but they do not know where to find it. They are convinced that they need more Bible study, but they are not satisfied with the conventional approaches, either of the Sunday School lessons or of the devotional manuals.

Robert Louis Stevenson maintained that if a man were to make a certain effort of imagination and would read the gospel "freshly like a book, not droningly and dully like a portion of the Bible, it would startle and move anyone." Perhaps the famous teller of tales was right. But, if Stevenson *was* right, it is necessary for us to find a concrete way in which the ordinary seeker can be helped to make his own experiment. To provide means to this end is the purpose of the present book. The proposal is that we try to confront Jesus Christ, as though for the first time. Sooner or later every person, if he means seriously to try to understand his world, must face the fact of Jesus Christ. So important is Christ for human history that all people, whether they count themselves His followers or not, must reckon with His existence. A life lived in Palestine nearly two thousand years ago determines the date of every secular document which men sign, and influences, directly or indirectly, countless human decisions. Christ can be accepted; He can be rejected; He cannot reasonably be ignored.

Important as Christ is, for both His friends and His enemies, there are millions who have never confronted Him in any direct way. They know a few phrases from His lips, but that is about all. Most Christians know individual stories from the Four Gospels, and they know a few scattered texts, but many have never gone straight through one of the books. We are very fortunate that these books exist, because they provide us with our best opportunity to confront Jesus Christ. Readers of *The Imitation of Christ* may remember how, in Book I, Chapter 1 of that priceless classic, we are advised to concentrate upon Christ as revealed in the gospels. "Let our foremost resolve," says à Kempis, "be to meditate upon the Life of Jesus Christ."

This book is an effort to help contemporary readers to obey the injunction of five hundred years ago. The method adopted is that of presenting in full the oldest gospel, the one attributed to Mark, each passage being accompanied with a brief interpretation. Because the purpose is frankly devotional, the interpretations are not intended as scholarly efforts, though it is hoped that nothing in them is inconsistent with the best Biblical scholarship. Actually it is not the scholarly effort which is most needed now, for that has been well done for a hundred years, so well done, in fact, that a virtual concensus has emerged. In regard to the three gospels which are called Synoptic, because they can be seen together in parallel columns, there is substantial agreement concerning literary authorship. It is agreed, for example, that Mark's is the basic gospel, preceding the two other synoptists, Matthew and Luke, and that other written sources were available to these writers. The contemporary reader is fortunate in that a number of first-rate scholars have taken the trouble to provide the general public with intelligible accounts of the main results of New Testament studies, dealing with the probable origin, composition, authorship, and date of the various books. In regard to the earliest gospel no living author has been more helpful than Professor H. G. Wood, of Birmingham, England, particularly in his essay on "The Life and Teaching of Jesus," and his commentary on Mark, in Peake's *Commentary on the Bible*. A most valuable work on Mark is that of B. Harvie Branscomb, whose study is one unit of the Moffatt Commentary. The reader who seeks the help of the most thorough scholarship would consult Vincent Taylor's *The Gospel According to Mark*.

What is needed, at this juncture, is an effort to understand the gospel account by meditation in depth. Almost every line can lead to a genuine enrichment of our lives, providing we proceed without hurry and with a sense of fresh encounter. The surprising result is that many sentences, which we have known superficially since childhood, suddenly take on new or even startling meaning. The method is to concentrate upon each part singly, though in continuity, in order to see what each sentence *means*. The effort is wonderfully justified in its effect on the inner life of the thoughtful and reverent reader.

By limiting our present study to Mark's gospel we necessarily omit some elements of undoubted greatness, such as the story of the Good Samaritan or the Sermon on the Mount, but we have the essentials in the briefest form. We do not, of course, have a full biography of Christ or a complete record of His sayings. These we shall never have. What we do have is a swiftly moving account of what one first-century Christian thought was sufficient for an avowedly evangelistic purpose. His intention was to make readers believe in Jesus as the Son of God. All seems selected to that end. The expected readers are Gentiles, that is, people like most of us. Papias, Bishop of Hierapolis in Asia Minor, wrote about A.D. 125, "Mark, having become the interpreter of Peter, wrote down accurately everything that he remembered, without, however, recording in order what was either said or done by Christ." We have reason to be immeasurably grateful for what Mark did, even though, as Papias indicated, he did not produce a fully ordered biography. The degree to which the other gospel writers honored Mark's effort is indicated by the fact that the substance of approximately two-thirds of Mark is reproduced by *both* Matthew and Luke and the remaining one-third, except for thirty verses, is reproduced by either Matthew or Luke. The whole of Mark, except for fifty-five verses, appears in Matthew.

The system of chapters of the New Testament now in

general use was invented by Cardinal Hugo de S. Caro in 1238. Our division into verses, which is in many ways unfortunate, was introduced by Robertus Stephanus in 1551, after the popularization of printing. When we realize that the now conventional divisions are comparatively modern, being no part of the original, we are free to try to make an improvement on them in order to present the gospel in its natural units. Since the chapters of the gospel, as ordinarily printed, are far too long for daily use, and since each includes too many topics, it is hoped that the present division into sixty short sections will constitute an improvement, so far as the average reader is concerned. To assist identification, the familiar chapter-and-verse notation is given at the end of each of the new units.

"Meditate on His life," wrote à Kempis, "and thou wilt be ashamed to find how far removed thou art from His perfection." Real confrontation should involve all that is needed in devotional experience. It should emphasize both our unworthiness and our hope, both our separation from God and our potential reconciliation. It is almost impossible to confront Christ without consequent prayer, and the experience is not likely to be long continued without real amendment of life.

I

The Preparation

The beginning of the gospel of Jesus Christ, the Son of God.

As it is written in Isaiah the prophet,
"Behold, I send my messenger before thy face,
who shall prepare thy way;
the voice of one crying in the wilderness:
Prepare the way of the Lord,
make his paths straight—"

John the baptizer appeared in the wilderness, preaching a baptism of repentance for the forgiveness of sins. And there went out to him all the country of Judea, and all the people of Jerusalem; and they were baptized by him in the river Jordan, confessing their sins. Now John was clothed with camel's hair, and had a leather girdle around his waist, and ate locusts and wild honey. And he preached, saying, "After me comes he who is mightier than I, the thong of whose sandals I am not worthy to stoop down and untie. I have baptized you with water; but he will baptize you with the Holy Spirit."

In those days Jesus came from Nazareth of Galilee and was baptized by John in the Jordan. And when he came up out of the water, immediately he saw the heavens opened and the Spirit descending upon him like a dove; and a voice came from heaven, "Thou art my beloved

Son; with thee I am well pleased."

The Spirit immediately drove him out into the wilderness. And he was in the wilderness forty days, tempted by Satan; and he was with the wild beasts; and the angels ministered to him. (1:1–13)

Christianity is centered, not primarily in ideas, but in events. It is based on what has actually occurred, rather than on some speculation which might be pleasing. If God is truly and deeply personal, as careful thought leads us to conclude, i.e., if He can honestly be addressed as "Thou," His clearest revelation must necessarily be in the life of a person. He cannot be accurately or fully revealed in the majesty of the stars or in the terror of the storm, but He can be thus revealed in a personal life of one who knows and suffers and cares. The good news, which unites all Christians of all generations, is that such a personal revelation has *occurred*. It has occurred in the context of ordinary history, in the life of a person who lived at at particular time and in a particular place.

The life of Jesus Christ came, not as a separate event, but as the climax of a particular historical process, without which His coming would have been unintelligible. Behind Him stood a whole succession of prophets, such as Isaiah and Jeremiah. The last of these, John, was essentially His contemporary. John the Baptist began a preparatory ministry in the fifteenth year of Tiberius, i.e., A.D. 26 or 27. The great creeds go out of their way to emphasize the concrete historical context of the Christian revelation. Indeed, both the Apostles' Creed and the Nicene Creed mention Pontius Pilate, the brutal and contemptuous Roman governor, who ruled A.D. 26–36. Christianity is not merely speculative, for it is firmly rooted in history.

John was, by any valid standard, a great man. He was the chief instrument of a genuine religious revival, yet humble enough to recognize that he was as nothing in comparison to his successor. He was trying to prepare aroused men and women for a new day of faith, in which reality would be the only test. Thus he minimized even the symbolic ceremony of baptism, by which we name him, saying that, in the great day coming, the emphasis would not be upon water, which is incidental, but upon the new life of God in men's hearts. This he called baptism by the Holy Spirit.

Jesus, by sharing in John's baptism, identified Himself with the sinful people whom He came to save. His experience with the fiery prophet of the wilderness became the historical occasion for His clarified consciousness of His own divine vocation. The sense of wonder which this recognition brought was so acute that Jesus felt the need of engaging in a long retreat alone, in order to see more clearly what His destined way might be.

2

The Threefold Ministry

Now after John was arrested, Jesus came into Galilee, preaching the gospel of God, and saying, "The time is fulfilled, and the kingdom of God is at hand; repent, and believe in the gospel."

And passing along by the Sea of Galilee, he saw Simon and Andrew the brother of Simon casting a net in the sea; for they were fishermen. And Jesus said to them, "Follow me and I will make you become fishers of men." And immediately they left their nets and followed him. And going on a little farther, he saw James the son of Zebedee and John his brother, who were in their boat mending the nets. And immediately he called them; and they left their father Zebedee in the boat with the hired servants, and followed him.

And they went into Capernaum; and immediately on the sabbath he entered the synagogue and taught. And they were astonished at his teaching, for he taught them as one who had authority, and not as the scribes. And immediately there was in their synagogue a man with an unclean spirit; and he cried out, "What have you to do with us, Jesus of Nazareth? Have you come to destroy us? I know who you are, the Holy One of God." But Jesus rebuked him, saying, "Be silent, and come out of him!" And the unclean spirit, convulsing him and crying with

4

a loud voice, came out of him. And they were all amazed, so that they questioned among themselves, saying, "What is this? A new teaching! With authority he commands even the unclean spirits, and they obey him." And at once his fame spread everywhere throughout all the surrounding region of Galilee. (1:14–28)

The importance of the influence of John in Christ's life is hard to exaggerate. As John's preaching became the occasion of the sense of divine call, so John's imprisonment was the event which inspired the beginning of Christ's public ministry. Whereas, in the baptism experience, it was revealed to Christ that He was the Coming One whom John predicted, it was the moral injustice of John's arrest and imprisonment which provided the necessary impetus for the start of a career of public witness. Jesus did not, it appears, begin to preach as soon as the Temptation was ended nor, in any case, did He return at once to Galilee. John's arrest, which was tragic, was turned into a victory, in that Christ could no longer work in close association with the fiery prophet and had to start His own public career.

As Christ came into Galilee, He exhibited at once all of the major elements of His ministry. These elements were three. In the first place, He proclaimed a message. What made this remarkable was its mood and tense. The mood was personal and urgent. The consequence is that we are told relatively little of what Christ said on those early occasions, but much of how He said it. Christ did not begin by telling of the glorious acts of God in the past, nor of the glittering hope of the future. Instead He spoke of the living, immediate *present.* "The time," He said, "is fulfilled." Such a message, given with burning passion, is inevitably exciting because the completed present is the most moving of all tenses. The past is irretrievably gone and the future may never be, but the present is vivid and real. The good news started with the message of *God in the present tense.*

The second element of Christ's ministry, which appeared in the opening scene, was the direct calling of individual men. He needed helpers and He found them early. The primary extension of Christ's kingdom comes when men and women are reached one by one, as occurred in the recruitment of the unlearned fishermen of Galilee. There is no reason to suppose that these four men, Simon, Andrew, James, and John, were seeing Jesus for the first time, but the call to participation was undoubtedly fresh and new. It was given with such confidence that it was answered without hesitation.

The third characteristic element of Christ's ministry, which appeared at the beginning, was that of *healing.* Exactly how He healed we do not know, but it is unhistorical to stress Christ's teaching without equal emphasis upon release from human suffering. We cannot present Christ accurately if we present Him merely as Teacher, or Leader, or Healer, for He was all three, and He was all three all the time. The pattern appeared early and was continually repeated.

3

Christ at Prayer

And immediately he left the synagogue, and entered the house of Simon and Andrew, with James and John. Now Simon's mother-in-law lay sick with a fever, and immediately they told him of her. And he came and took her by the hand and lifted her up, and the fever left her; and she served them.

That evening, at sundown, they brought to him all who were sick or possessed with demons. And the whole city was gathered together about the door. And he healed many who were sick with various diseases, and cast out many demons; and he would not permit the demons to speak, because they knew him.

And in the morning, a great while before day, he rose and went out to a lonely place, and there he prayed. And Simon and those who were with him followed him, and they found him and said to him, "Every one is searching for you." And he said to them, "Let us go on to the next towns, that I may preach there also; for that is why I came out." And he went throughout all Galilee, preaching in their synagogues and casting out demons.

And a leper came to him beseeching him, and kneeling said to him, "If you will, you can make me clean." Moved with pity, he stretched out his hand and touched him, and said to him, "I will; be clean." And immediately the leprosy left him, and he was made clean. And he sternly charged him, and sent him away at once, and said to him, "See that you say nothing to any one; but go, show yourself to the priest, and offer for your cleansing what Moses commanded, for a proof to the people." But he went out and began to talk freely about it, and to spread the news, so that Jesus could no longer openly enter a town, but was out in the country; and people came to him from every quarter. (1:29–45)

From the beginning, Christ's concern was not merely for the nation in general, but for the needs of individual persons. The earliest followers lived in ordinary families in which ordinary illnesses occurred. Therefore it was wholly appropriate that, when Christ went from the synagogue on the Sabbath to the home of Simon, He should give attention to Simon's mother-in-law, who was ill with a fever. The immediate cure of this woman, with whom Christ had a personal connection, led naturally to the coming of many other distressed people, each of whom He apparently dealt with individually, even though the previous connection was not so close.

Many of those who were relieved of their distresses were said to have been possessed of demons. Exactly what this means we do not know, but we are keenly aware of the fact, which we observe in contemporary experience, that many people act as though they are driven by forces which they cannot control. The changing terminology which we use to designate a particular misfortune or illness is not as important as is the fact that relief can come. No interpretation of Christianity, which omits the possibility of such actual healing, is valid. Though we assume today, without question, that the belief in demons is entirely illusory, our assumption is itself highly questionable. We do not know enough to make such a flat rejection. What we do know is that Christ changed the lives of countless warped personalities and that He did so by the contagious assurance, illustrated in His own character, of the reality of God's protection.

The second scene in this act, which started in the synagogue at Capernaum, was Christ's voluntary retirement. After the terrific outpouring of compassion, He felt the need of being alone in prayer. Consequently He made Himself deliberately unavailable to the needy people, not because He failed to care for them, but because, even in His life, the inner wells had to have time to be refilled. The fact that Jesus prayed is a fact of transcendent importance in our effort to know who He was. His resort to prayer indicates His own humility and His personal sense of need. What this means is that, though Jesus accurately revealed God the Father, He was not God the Father. The fact that He did not feel self-sufficient was one mark of His divine vocation. Furthermore, the fact that He prayed makes His life more relevant to ours. Prayer is something which He and we have in common.

4

Forgiveness of the Unworthy

And when he returned to Capernaum after some days, it was reported that he was at home. And many were gathered together, so that there was no longer room for them, not even about the door; and he was preaching the word to them. And they came, bringing to him a paralytic carried by four men. And when they could not get near him because of the crowd, they removed the roof above him; and when they had made an opening, they let down the pallet on which the paralytic lay. And when Jesus saw their faith, he said to the paralytic, "My son, your sins are forgiven." Now some of the scribes were sitting there, questioning in their hearts. "Why does this man speak thus? It is blasphemy! Who can forgive sins but God alone?" And immediately Jesus, perceiving in his spirit that they thus questioned within themselves, said to them, "Why do you question thus in your hearts? Which is easier, to say to the paralytic, 'Your sins are forgiven,' or to say, 'Rise, take up your pallet and walk'? But that you may know that the Son of man has authority on earth to forgive sins"—he said to the paralytic—"I say to you, rise, take up your pallet and go home." And he rose, and immediately took up the pallet and went out before them all; so that they were all amazed and glorified God, saying, "We never saw anything like this!" (2:1–12)

Among the incidents of healing, some were more significant than others. One of the most significant concerned a paralyzed man who was healed in Capernaum. The significance lay in the fact that the condition of release was a sense of forgiveness, and this Christ gave the poor man in the most explicit terms. Sensing that the man was harassed by unresolved feelings of guilt, Christ began by telling him that his sins were already forgiven.

It is clear that the assertion of forgiveness was even more offensive to the Pharisees than was Christ's message of the Kingdom or even His acts of healing. Forgiveness, especially when applied to the obviously unworthy, is a direct threat to any purely legal system. It plays havoc with any conception of the necessity of equality between deeds and punishment. The scribes, when they heard the assertion of forgiveness, faced only two alternatives; either they had to declare unending war on Christ or they had to learn to say humbly with the publican of the parable, "God be merciful to me a sinner." Their decision was to declare war, a war which led ultimately to the crucifixion, and their first warlike act was to accuse Jesus of blasphemy.

Christianity is meaningless apart from the centrality of forgiveness. The Kingdom of Christ is not for the good and righteous people, though forms of goodness are a result of it, but rather for the people who know that they are not good. The gospel does not say, as we tend to say today, "Be good, and you will become worthy of meeting God." It says, instead, "Repent, and unacceptable as you may be, you are accepted." A religion which demands concrete evidence of goodness as a precondition of salvation is a religion of impossible burden. Consequently Christ makes no such demand, but begins with sinners as they are. If forgiveness is real, each life can make a new redemptive start each day.

There are people who say they do not need to make a vocal witness, because, as they express it, they "just let their lives speak." This appears as humility, but is really self-righteousness. No person's life is good enough to speak with any adequacy. Christ, Himself, indicated this when He put into His pattern prayer the phrase, "Forgive us our sins as we forgive those who sin against us." He expected this prayer to be endlessly necessary, so long as we are in this life. The entrance into Christ's Kingdom is by the continual rebirth of the sinner into the fellowship of the forgiven. The redemptive fellowship, on which Christ necessarily depends, is made up of those whose first qualification for membership is the recognition that they are unworthy of membership.

5

The Boldness of Christ

He went out again beside the sea; and all the crowd gathered about him, and he taught them. And as he passed on, he saw Levi the son of Alphaeus sitting at the tax office, and he said to him, "Follow me." And he rose and followed him.

And as he sat at table in his house, many tax collectors and sinners were sitting with Jesus and his disciples; for there were many who followed him. And the scribes of the Pharisees, when they saw that he was eating with sinners and tax collectors, said to his disciples. "Why does he eat with tax collectors and sinners?" And when Jesus heard it, he said to them, "Those who are well have no need of a physician, but those who are sick; I came not to call the righteous, but sinners."

Now John's disciples and the Pharisees were fasting; and people came and said to him, "Why do John's disciples and the disciples of the Pharisees fast, but your disciples do not fast?" And Jesus said to them, "Can the wedding guests fast while the bridegroom is with them? As long as they have the bridegroom with them, they cannot fast. The days will come, when the bridegroom is taken away from them, and then they will fast in that day. No one sews a piece of unshrunk cloth on an old garment; if he does, the patch tears away from it, the new from the old, and a worse tear is made. And no one puts new wine into old wineskins; if he does, the wine will burst the skins, and the wine is lost, and so are the skins; but new wine is for fresh skins." (2:13–22)

In calling the fishermen as His recruits, Christ was breaking with established religious practice, for these men were unschooled and in no sense professionally religious. The calling of Levi was, however, an even more striking departure. This was because Levi had become, by the very nature of his work, unpopular with his neighbors. The fact that the man was a tax gatherer meant that he, though a Jew, was closely allied to the Roman tyranny. His position was somewhat like that of a collaborator in the language of contemporary struggles. But Christ defied popular opinion in order to secure a man whom He needed.

This boldness was even more pronounced in Christ's social life. Christ shocked the devout by deliberately associating, not only with tax collectors, but with other people who had broken with narrowly sectarian or nationalistic practices. He chose, moreover, to gather with those who were conspicuously careless of the Law. We are not surprised that the Pharisees were outraged when we realize that the idea of maintaining holiness through separation is involved in their name itself. Christ's bold action represented a genuine departure from a received conception of what religion means, in His determination to seek out sinners, rather than to avoid them. His interest was in the welfare of broken and needy men, not in the trivial determination to keep His own skirts clean or His reputation unsullied. It was as though, living in a Nevada town, He would deliberately enter the gambling houses to be where the people are, regardless of what the stricter neighbors might think or say.

The story of mingling happily with those who were not strict in observances introduces a real contrast with John, as well as with the Pharisees. John and the Pharisees agreed on one thing, the necessity of fasting, but Christ, by contrast, made men feel that they were partaking of a marriage feast. They were keeping a festival rather than a fast, because God was, indeed, appearing to His people. The tragedy of the cross is still in the future, but even this will be a victory. Christ's religion was shocking partly because it was fundamentally gay.

All this means that Christ represents a radically new departure in the life of faith. It is so new that it cannot be successfully patched on to something old and fundamentally dissimilar. It is so different from any antecedent faith that it may be accurately compared to new wine, which, as it works, will break any containers, unless they are likewise new.

6

The Standard of Judgment

One sabbath he was going through the grainfields; and as they made their way his disciples began to pluck ears of grain. And the Pharisees said to him, "Look, why are they doing what is not lawful on the sabbath?" And he said to them, "Have you never read what David did, when he was in need and was hungry, he and those who were with him: how he entered the house of God, when Abiathar was high priest, and ate the bread of the Presence, which it is not lawful for any but the priests to eat, and also gave it to those who were with him?" And he said to them, "The sabbath was made for man, not man for the sabbath; so the Son of man is lord even of the sabbath."

Again he entered the synagogue, and a man was there who had a withered hand. And they watched him, to see whether he would heal him on the sabbath, so that they might accuse him. And he said to the man who had the withered hand, "Come here." And he said to them, "Is it lawful on the sabbath to do good or to do harm, to save life or to kill?" But they were silent. And he looked around at them with anger, grieved at their hardness of heart, and said to the man, "Stretch out your hand." He stretched it out, and his hand was restored. The Pharisees went out, and immediately held counsel with the Herodians against him, how to destroy him. (2:23–3:6)

At no point was Christ's conflict with the religious establishment clearer than in regard to Sabbath observance. It is no wonder that the Jewish authorities honored the Sabbath, for this was one of the ways in which a peculiar people had been able to maintain itself, while they were surrounded by pagan peoples who recognized no such regular rhythm between work and reverent rest. The rhythm of the week was an important asset and has proved to be so in every region of the world where it has been introduced. Christ was by no means opposed to the honoring of the Sabbath, but He was clearly opposed to a way of life in which strictness of observance conflicted with other and greater values. The meeting of elemental human need, He maintained, is a more serious ethical demand than is a rule about a day. He countered conservatism by appealing to an older conservatism, that of David the King.

In this conflict we reach something akin to a philosophy, in that the specific problem is settled by reference to an enduring principle. The principle involved is that the final test of any practice consists in what it does to people. People are not only more important than *things:* they are also more important than *rules,* for rules are intrinsically instrumental. If rules, in the long run, make human life better they are worth keeping, but if not, they are to be discarded. The danger, Jesus saw, lies in our temptation to make an idol out of something which was never intended to be anything but a means.

Once this principle was enunciated in an unforgettable way, Christ was ready to put it to the test by reference to a problem more serious than mere hunger, the problem of physical disability. Accordingly, being in the synagogue on the Sabbath, He proceeded boldly to heal a man who suffered with a withered hand. In response to the latent or vocal criticism of those who supposed religion to be a matter of specific rules, Christ was by no means calm, but blazed out in anger. This is only one of many instances which demonstrates that our modern stereotype of "gentle Jesus meek and mild" is completely false. Christ's obvious anger in the face of the pious elevation of something other than human need, and His bold action in the face of criticism, solidified the opposition to Him.

7

The Redemptive Fellowship

Jesus withdrew with his disciples to the sea, and a great multitude from Galilee followed; also from Judea and Jerusalem and Idumea and from beyond the Jordan and from about Tyre and Sidon a great multitude, hearing all that he did, came to him. And he told his disciples to have a boat ready for him because of the crowd, lest they should crush him; for he had healed many, so that all who had diseases pressed upon him to touch him. And whenever the unclean spirits beheld him, they fell down before him and cried out, "You are the Son of God." And he strictly ordered them not to make him known.

And he went up into the hills, and called to him those whom he desired; and they came to him. And he appointed twelve, to be with him, and to be sent out to preach and have authority to cast out demons: Simon whom he surnamed Peter; James the Son of Zebedee and John the brother of James, whom he surnamed Boanerges, that is, sons of thunder; Andrew, and Philip, and Bartholomew, and Matthew, and Thomas, and James the son of Alphaeus, and Thaddaeus, and Simon the Cananaean, and Judas Iscariot, who betrayed him. (3:7–19)

From the beginning of His public ministry Christ had disciples. These were the people who were, in one sense,

His students. They listened gladly, they went with Him into the synagogues, they observed sympathetically His acts of healing, and some followed Him wherever He went. They were not closely organized, but they were distinguishable from the crowds which were essentially temporary combinations of people, many appearing only once. It soon became obvious that Christ had no real hope in the crowds. They gathered, largely because of His reputation as a healer of diseases, often to gaze in wonder at a new and diverting sight. Their presence was no indication of a deep commitment. Consequently they could not be counted upon in a crisis. Crowds may be inevitable in a new redemptive movement, but it is not on the multitude that any movement can be built. Indeed, the passing popularity can be a genuine barrier. Christ deliberately tried to limit His popularity by warning those whom He helped against making the help known.

As Christ's holy vocation became clear, He decided to make the crucial step of creating a hard core of committed workers, the Twelve. He saw that, while the crowds might come and go, they would certainly provide no support in a crisis. Indeed, they might easily turn, like any mob, in the other direction and call for the crucifixion of the very One whom, earlier, they had so much admired. If the movement, on which the redemption of the world depended, were to continue after His physical death, the only alternative was to produce a little band, as disciplined that of Gideon, and consequently able to pierce the defenses of the surrounding pagan world. The broad weapon would surely fail, but the hard, sharp one might be able to penetrate. Since there was no valid hope in crowds, and since the witness of the lone individual would always be lost, the only alternative was the formation of the small redemptive group. The strategy of Christ was the strategy of dependence upon the hard core.

In forming His group, on whom so much depended, Christ had to use ordinary people. The rock on which He built His church was the rubble of common human nature. Clearly He did select, since we know that the number of disciples far exceeded the number of the Twelve, but even those whom He selected turned out to be dismally weak in times of stress. Simon proved to be a coward, after all his boasting; Judas was a traitor; and the sons of Zebedee were crassly self-seeking; yet the miracle was that the fellowship endured. By means of the Twelve, Christ changed the history of the world. Unworthy and incompetent as these men were, there was something about their association with one another and with Christ which made them able to endure and to conquer, while the contemporary power of Rome went into decay. Herein is the primary miracle.

8

The Charge of Insanity

Then he went home; and the crowd came together again, so that they could not even eat. And when his friends heard it, they went out to seize him, for they said, "He is beside himself." And the scribes who came down from Jerusalem said, "He is possessed by Beelzebul, and by the prince of demons he casts out the demons." And he called them to him, and said to them in parables, "How can Satan cast out Satan? If a kingdom is divided against itself, that kingdom cannot stand. And if a house is divided against itself, that house will not be able to stand. And if Satan has risen up against himself and is divided, he cannot stand, but is coming to an end. But no one can enter a strong man's house and plunder his goods, unless he first binds the strong man; then indeed he may plunder his house.

"Truly, I say to you, all sins will be forgiven the sons of men, and whatever blasphemies they utter; but whoever blasphemes against the Holy Spirit never has forgiveness, but is guilty of an eternal sin"—for they had said, "He has an unclean spirit."

And his mother and his brothers came; and standing outside they sent to him and called him. And a crowd was sitting about him; and they said to him, "Your mother and your brothers are outside, asking for you." And he replied, "Who are my mother and my brothers?" And looking around on those who sat about him, he said, "Here are my mother and my brothers! Whoever does the will of God is my brother, and sister, and mother." (3:20–35)

It is not very surprising that many people, when they contemplated the boldness and unconventionality of Christ, believed that He was insane. How else, on their premises, could they account for His carelessness about His personal reputation and His manifest intensity. The smart thing to do is to accept religion, but to accept it mildly and make no great fuss about it. Since Christ departed so vividly from the popular course, and since He took the present reign of God so seriously, He was obviously unbalanced. A man who takes such an interest in unbalanced people must be a little unbalanced himself. Men are drawn to the practice of psychiatry, we say in our unkind way, because they need it.

What is striking is the way in which the diagnosis of Christ's mental illness was made equally by friends and enemies. It was His friends who tried to seize Him because they thought He was distraught, and this opinion was evidently shared by His own mother and brothers, Mary's younger children, for they came to get Him. Clearly they were embarrassed, and their purpose was to save Him, to give Him a period of rest, in which He could become restored to normalcy. Christ resisted His family, not because He failed to love them, but because His area of affection was so wide.

The enemies, accepting uncritically the conception of

demon possession, asserted that His great success in liberating the possessed arose from the fact that He was Himself possessed in an extreme fashion. To this charge Jesus replied, with marked sanity, in what may be recognized as the spirit of Socrates, that is, by the appeal to consistency. The notion of evil curing evil is a contradiction in terms. Error does not overcome error; it is overcome only by truth. The very ability to heal the possessed indicates, therefore, a fundamental soundness of mind.

There is a sin, said Christ, which, so long as it goes on, is intrinsically unforgivable, in that it closes the mind to the very possibility of redemption. Those who are so sure of their own righteousness that they deliberately close their minds to any disturbing truth have an impenetrable defense against the divine disturbance. Blasphemy against the Holy Spirit is not a particular use of words, nor even a particular act, but the attitude of self-righteousness which automatically closes the mind. The sin that is intrinsically unforgivable is the complacency which keeps a man from hearing the divine knocking at his door.

9

Teaching by Parables

Again he began to teach beside the sea. And a very large crowd gathered about him, so that he got into a boat and sat in it on the sea; and the whole crowd was beside the sea on the land. And he taught them many things in parables, and in his teaching he said to them: "Listen! A sower went out to sow. And as he sowed, some seed fell along the path, and the birds came and devoured it. Other seed fell on rocky ground, where it had not much soil, and immediately it sprang up, since it had no depth of soil; and when the sun rose it was scorched, and since it had no root it withered away. Other seed fell among thorns and the thorns grew up and choked it, and it yielded no grain. And other seeds fell into good soil and brought forth grain, growing up and increasing and yielding thirtyfold and sixtyfold and a hundredfold." And he said, "He who has ears to hear, let him hear."

And when he was alone, those who were about him with the twelve asked him concerning the parables. And he said to them, "To you has been given the secret of the kingdom of God, but for those outside everything is in parables; so that they may indeed see but not perceive, and may indeed hear but not understand; lest they should turn again, and be forgiven." And he said to them, "Do you not understand this parable? How then will you understand all the parables?" (4:1–13)

Once the strategy of preparing the Twelve was accepted, a period of intensive training was inevitable. Though some of the messages given in this period were heard by the crowds, the explanations, as in the Parable of the Soils, were given to the Twelve in seclusion. What was required was a clear understanding of the nature of the Kingdom, because the Kingdom, as Christ meant it, was so different from what was involved in most of the popular Messianic expectations. Christ accordingly found it necessary to use a new teaching device, the parable. Though the parables have some literary ancestry, in the enigmatic sayings of the scribes, they are, as used in the New Testament, a novel literary form.

The Parable of the Soils is at once both a teaching in its own right and an illustration of Christ's general practice. Christ employed, in His teaching, familiar scenes, many of them agricultural, showing in each case something in the spiritual life which matched what was already known in the common life of everyday experience. Parables are not possible unless there is a deep sense in which God is the God of all life; He must be "Lord of heaven and earth" as well as "Father." He reigns in the present as truly as in the future, and He reigns in the wheat field as truly as in the synagogue. Many of the parables illustrate God's sovereignty, but they would not even be meaningful if that sovereignty were not already a recognized fact.

Fertility depends, not merely upon the vitality of the seed, but also upon the nature of the reception. The grace of receiving is quite as important as is the grace of giving. Just as good seeds are wasted in unreceptive ground, so a valid message is lost if there is not adequate effort on the part of the hearer.

It is not reasonable to conclude that Christ used parables in order to *increase* the perplexity and misunderstanding of those who rejected Him. Though the quotation from Isaiah 6:9–10 seems to give credence to this view, Christ's own subsequent words, about the light being put on the lamp stand, appear to be used deliberately to clear up misunderstanding on this point. The ultimate purpose, says Christ, is not concealment but clarity. People may fail to see, but when they do, their failure is no part of Christ's purpose. If we place this chapter in the context of the entire gospel, we are forced to conclude that Jesus used parables not *that*, "seeing, they may not see," but *because*, "seeing, they do not see."

10

Responsibility of the Listener

"The sower sows the word. And these are the ones along the path, where the word is sown; when they hear, Satan immediately comes and takes away the word which is sown in them. And these in like manner are the ones sown upon rocky ground, who, when they hear the word, immediately receive it with joy; and they have no root in themselves, but endure for a while; then, when tribulation or persecution arises on account of the word, immediately they fall away. And others are the ones sown among thorns; they are those who hear the word, but the cares of the world, and the delight in riches, and the desire for other things, enter in and choke the word, and it proves unfruitful. But those that were sown upon the good soil are the ones who hear the word and accept it and bear fruit, thirtyfold and sixtyfold and a hundred-fold."

And he said to them, "Is a lamp brought in to be put under a bushel, or under a bed, and not on a stand? For there is nothing hid, except to be made manifest; nor is anything secret, except to come to light. If any man has ears to hear, let him hear." And he said to them, "Take heed what you hear; the measure you give will be the measure you get, and still more will be given you. For to him who has will more be given; and from him who has not, even what he has will be taken away." (4:14–25)

Always it takes at least two to get the truth told. The task of the teller is a serious one, but the task of the listener is an equally great one. Because it is conventional to emphasize the responsibility of the one who tries to make a point clear, either publicly or privately, Christ does not need to stress this side of the fundamental transaction; He stresses, instead, the side of the receiver. The person who listens to a lecture and comes out disgruntled, saying he sees nothing in it, may be making a just estimate of the speaker, but also he may not. He may, instead, be telling something deeply damaging about himself. There is a sense in which every judgment is a self-judgment.

The humorous side of judgment is illustrated in the experience of the student who returns to college, listens to his old professor, and remarks consequently on the way in which the professor has grown. Actually, of course, the message as given is the same message, but it is the student who has grown. In his sophomore or rebellious mood he may not really hear, because hearing is a great deal more than a physical response. Hearing is as much an art as is speaking.

The parable of the soils, when interpreted by Christ, shows that there are many conditions which may limit receptivity. Words can be wasted, pearls can be cast before swine, the great word can be missed in the babble of little voices. Man's task, therefore, is that of keeping open and of not putting up impenetrable barriers. The fact that the room seems dark does not mean that there is not a light in the room; it may mean, instead, that the light has been deliberately closed off from effectiveness by the use of an opaque covering. It is not sufficient to have a light; it is equally necessary to put oneself into a position in which the light, if it exists, can be seen.

Because hearing is a serious business, Christ tells us to take heed what we hear. Failure to hear may be a revelation of obtuseness. Often the answer to the person who says he doesn't hear is that such failure is his own fault. And such failure can become a habit, so that it feeds upon itself. The longer we go without trying to be sensitive in our listening the harder it is to change. The barriers we raise become increasingly impenetrable, the longer we hide behind them.

Christ was never under the illusion that all who heard Him would understand, or would care or respond. He recognized that the clear profundity of His message would become a means of condemnation. But it was not Christ who condemned; it was the perverse listeners who condemned themselves.

I I

The Power of Small Beginnings

And he said, "The kingdom of God is as if a man should scatter seed upon the ground, and should sleep and rise night and day, and the seed should sprout and grow, he knows not how. The earth produces of itself, first the blade, then the ear, then the full grain in the ear. But when the grain is ripe, at once he puts in the sickle, because the harvest has come."

And he said, "With what can we compare the kingdom of God, or what parable shall we use for it? It is like a grain of mustard seed, which, when sown upon the ground, is the smallest of all the seeds on earth; yet when it is sown it grows up and becomes the greatest of all shrubs, and puts forth large branches, so that the birds of the air can make nests in its shade."

With many such parables he spoke the word to them, as they were able to hear it; he did not speak to them without a parable, but privately to his own disciples he explained everything. (4:26–34)

In His intense effort to make His message clear to the Twelve, Christ used a great many parables, most of which, apparently, were never written down and which are accordingly lost so far as we are concerned. Mark says Christ used a parable every time He spoke to the group. Though we may well be sad when we think about the parables that are forever lost, we have reason to be grateful that so many were saved. One of these, that of the seed which grows while the sower is asleep, is unique to Mark's account. If the earliest gospel had been discarded, on the ground that most of it had already been incorporated in the accounts of Matthew and Luke, this one would have been lost. It is a valuable teaching, in that it shows that ours is the kind of world in which growth can occur apart from the action of the initiator. Not all is dependent upon the efforts of feeble humanity. God has made the kind of world in which things *grow*. If this were not so, none of our efforts would suffice. We live in a world which has much of evil, but it is also a world in which we can count on redemptive influences, because the whole world is God's world.

The redemptive influences are not often those which, in the beginning, seem impressive or large. God works, pre-eminently, through small things, which, rightly handled, have great consequences. The scene which Christ had before Him as He taught this lesson has become the world's most impressive demonstration of its truth. Here was a tiny movement, entirely trivial in appearance, when contrasted with the legal and military and material might of the Roman Empire. But Christ put His faith in the little redemptive fellowship which was so small that it seemed insignificant to Roman contemporaries. Yet the truth is that the empire which Pilate and Herod represented came to an end, while the poor little fellowship, which could reasonably be compared to a tiny seed, lived on and lives still. It penetrated the culture of Greece and Rome and, when they decayed, it lived on through all changes of culture.

In the parable of the mustard seed, Christ tells us how the world is remade. It is not remade primarily by external forces, but by ideas and movements which affect human history because they have the power to convince and to change lives accordingly. In order to endure and to be effective the small group does not need to be made up of perfect men and women. The fellowship of weak and unworthy men can eventually be world-shaking, provided it is centered in the life of Christ.

The entire subsequent history of Christianity has been a remarkable vindication of the truth of Christ's teaching about the power of small beginnings. It has, indeed, been a miracle of history more striking than any one miracle performed by Jesus in His earthly career. The beginnings were pitifully small, wholly devoid of any of the elements of power which seem important in the world. There was, for example, no military or academic or financial strength. But the extended fellowship outlived the political and academic and military institutions which were contemporary with it. It is still alive today.

12

Storms Physical and Spiritual

On that day, when evening had come, he said to them, "Let us go across to the other side." And leaving the crowd, they took him with them, just as he was, in the boat. And other boats were with him. And a great storm of wind arose, and the waves beat into the boat, so that the boat was already filling. But he was in the stern, asleep on the cushion; and they woke him and said to him, "Teacher, do you not care if we perish?" And he awoke and rebuked the wind, and said to the sea, "Peace! Be still!" And the wind ceased, and there was a great calm. He said to them, "Why are you afraid? Have you no faith?" And they were filled with awe, and said to one another, "Who then is this, that even wind and sea obey him?"

They came to the other side of the sea, to the country of the Gerasenes. And when he had come out of the boat, there met him out of the tombs a man with an unclean spirit, who lived among the tombs; and no one could bind him any more, even with a chain; for he had often been bound with fetters and chains, but the chains he wrenched apart, and the fetters he broke in pieces; and no one had the strength to subdue him. Night and day among the tombs and on the mountains he was always crying out, and bruising himself with stones. (4:35–5:5)

34

A considerable amount of Christ's time with the intimate group was spent in crossing back and forth over the Sea of Galilee. Such movement may be explained in part by the evident necessity of getting away from the crowds, and it may also be explained by the growing enmity of Herod. That Herod would associate Christ with John was natural. In any case, the time on the sea was important and became the occasion for teaching which otherwise might not have been given.

The present story is of one particular passage which involved a fierce and sudden storm, clearly endangering the lives of all concerned. That we have here a story as told originally by an eyewitness is indicated by the reference to the other little ships, as well as the detail that Jesus was asleep on a pillow in the back of the ship. Pouring out His energy as He did when He healed and taught and met crowds, Christ evidently had to take His rest when He could get it. The fact that He could sleep calmly while the squall was coming up shows, almost as well as the actual miracle of calming the waves, that He felt complete confidence in His Father's care.

If we really believe in God's ultimate sovereignty, by which we mean that the order of even the physical universe is the order of God's eternal purpose, we shall have no insuperable difficulty in accepting the account of the stilling of the storm. To suppose that God can control minds, but cannot control the forces of nature which are His handiwork, is to be a halfhearted and inconsistent believer. We do not know enough about the nature of the world to set arbitrary limits to the power of prayer.

In any case a Christian who prays regarding the weather, or for physical healing, or for any material change, is acting in accordance with the practice of Christ.

Stormy as the passage over the inland sea was, the events after landing on the eastern shore were stormier still. We are struck, again, with how little peace Christ was given. He could not cross the sea undisturbed, and He could not land without facing a bitter human problem. The problem in this case was that of a man obviously insane and consequently dangerous. The incident is indicative of how bad human tragedy can be. The man was so deranged that he was a peril to himself as well as to others. He represented a human situation which, to ordinary eyes, though not to the eyes of Christ, seemed utterly hopeless. The consequent drain or Christ's compassion was immense.

13

The Release of the Possessed

And when he saw Jesus from afar, he ran and worshiped him; and crying out with a loud voice, he said, "What have you to do with me, Jesus, Son of the Most High God? I adjure you by God, do not torment me." For he had said to him, "Come out of the man, you unclean spirit!" And Jesus asked him, "What is your name?" He replied, "My name is Legion; for we are many." And he begged him eagerly not to send them out of the country. Now a great herd of swine was feeding there on the hillside; and they begged him, "Send us to the swine, let us enter them." So he gave them leave. And the unclean spirits came out, and entered the swine; and the herd, numbering about two thousand, rushed down the steep bank into the sea, and were drowned in the sea.

The herdsmen fled, and told it in the city and in the country. And people came to see what it was that had happened. And they came to Jesus, and saw the demoniac sitting there, clothed and in his right mind, the man who had had the legion; and they were afraid. And those who had seen it told what had happened to the demoniac and to the swine. And they began to beg Jesus to depart from their neighborhood. And as he was getting into the boat, the man who had been possessed with demons begged him that he might be with him. But he refused, and said to him, "Go home to your friends, and tell them how much the Lord has done for you, and how he has had mercy on you." And he went away and began to proclaim in the Decapolis how much Jesus had done for him; and all men marveled. (5:5–20)

Something of the importance of the story of the Gadarene demoniac is indicated by the fact that, in Mark's rapid and condensed account, it is longer than most other stories. The encounter began by the insane man recognizing Christ as somehow different from the others and going straight to Him. Disturbed as he was, he recognized in Christ a new source of disturbance. He had learned to live in his terrible way and did not really want to have his life changed. He sensed, what many have sensed since, that Christ often brings a sword which cuts, before He provides a peace which calms and heals.

Christ's way of dealing with the deranged man was to attack the trouble at its source, that is, to try to eliminate the fears and hatreds which possessed him. Even the man, himself, understood perfectly that his damaging fears and hatreds were many rather than few. So wedded was he to his perverse life, that he was afraid he *would* be cured. Accordingly he asked that Christ not send his hatreds away; he had learned to enjoy them. In a sense he reveled in his bitterness.

What happened to cause disaster to the herd of swine we do not know. We may be assured, in any case, that Christ would not wantonly destroy the valuable property of another. Furthermore, the terrible things which possess men do not need, when they are eliminated in one place, to go to another. In Christ's care they can be utterly destroyed, so that henceforth they are nothing. It is possible that the pigs were frightened and thus wrought their own destruction. In that case, it could be accurately said that the same spirit of fear which had so nearly ruined the man had also ruined them.

In the end the man of Gadara became a symbol of what can happen to distraught men and women if they submit themselves to the influences of Christ's life. His derangement ended, he naturally wanted to go with the Twelve so that he could have the continuing effect of Christ's presence. But this was precisely what he was not permitted to do. The inner group had to remain small if it was to be effective. Furthermore the man, being a Gentile, could easily have a ministry of his own in his own familiar environment. It is easier to volunteer to go to some distant place of service, but Christ often calls men to make their witness in their own homes and in their regular work.

14

The Healing Touch

And when Jesus had crossed again in the boat to the other side, a great crowd gathered about him; and he was beside the sea. Then came one of the rulers of the synagogue, Jairus by name; and seeing him, he fell at his feet, and besought him, saying, "My little daughter is at the point of death. Come and lay your hands on her, so that she may be made well, and live." And he went with him.

And a great crowd followed him and thronged about him. And there was a woman who had had a flow of blood for twelve years, and who had suffered much under many physicians, and had spent all that she had, and was no better but rather grew worse. She had heard the reports about Jesus, and came up behind him in the crowd and touched his garment. For she said, "If I touch even his garments, I shall be made well." And immediately the hemorrhage ceased; and she felt in her body that she was healed of her disease. And Jesus, perceiving in himself that power had gone forth from him, immediately turned about in the crowd, and said, "Who touched my garments?" And his disciples said to him, "You see the crowd pressing around you, and yet you say, 'Who touched me?'." And he looked around to see who had done it. But the woman, knowing what had been done to her, came in fear and trembling and fell down before him, and told him the whole truth. And he said to her, "Daughter, your faith has made you well; go in peace, and be healed of your disease." (5:21–34)

How Jesus healed people we do not really know. That He did something, and that it seemed like work, is obvious from the fact that His critics were opposed to healing on the Sabbath, for it was work to which they objected. Often He said words which were helpful, but, in the case of the woman with an issue of blood, there were no words at all. The very proximity to Christ seems to have given the poor woman what she needed.

We get some idea of how numerous the acts of healing were when we see that one story, that of the poor woman, comes in the midst of another. Christ healed one while He was on the way to relieve a second sorrowful situation. We may be sure that the gospels tell only a few of the human stories, just as they include only a few of the parables. Because life can go wrong at so many points, there is no end to human tragedy and the needy cases will always press upon one another. Christ was gay with the publicans and sinners; He feasted rather than fasted; but He was also in constant touch with all kinds of pain and disappointment.

The woman who was healed so suddenly is representative of the many of this world who have ample reason for discouragement. Her physical disability had continued unabated for twelve long years, years in which she had gone to many physicians, but with each succeeding hope blasted. The consequence of much fruitless medical care was that she was impoverished as well as ill. She was only one out of a great throng about Jesus, but He, recognizing that a genuine contact had been made, sought the poor woman out, and treated her as an individual rather than merely a part of the faceless crowd.

The most remarkable feature of this appealing account of relief is that, according to Christ's own words, the healing agent was the woman's own faith. Christ did not consciously help her, because she was healed before He was aware of her presence, but she was healed because her faith was so great. As she gave herself, unreservedly, to the power which she felt in Christ's person, she became a new person, because faith is itself miraculous. Though we have absolutely no idea what the limits of a powerful faith may be, we must never let our faith be an end in itself. What the poor woman had was not faith in *faith:* she had faith in *Christ.* Faith is a word which requires an object. We recognize that mere faith is not an adequate answer to human ills, when we realize that we can have faith in that which is intrinsically unworthy. If we give full attention to Christ, we do not need to worry about the subjective effects. They will take care of themselves.

15

The Sleeping Child

While he was still speaking, there came from the ruler's house some who said, "Your daughter is dead. Why trouble the Teacher any further?" But ignoring what they said, Jesus said to the ruler of the synagogue, "Do not fear, only believe." And he allowed no one to follow him except Peter and James and John the brother of James. When they came to the house of the ruler of the synagogue, he saw a tumult, and people weeping and wailing loudly. And when he had entered, he said to them, "Why do you make a tumult and weep? The child is not dead but sleeping." And they laughed at him. But he put them all outside, and took the child's father and mother and those who were with him, and went in where the child was. Taking her by the hand he said to her, "Talitha cumi"; which means, "Little girl, I say to you, arise." And immediately the girl got up and walked; for she was twelve years old. And immediately they were overcome with amazement. And he strictly charged them that no one should know this, and told them to give her something to eat. (5:35–43)

Nearly every parent knows the powerful emotion connected with the severe illness of a child. Children's diseases were worse calamities in earlier days than they are now, as a visit to almost any old cemetery will verify. So great was the concern of one Jewish father that he paid no attention to the growing rift between Jesus and men of his type. Being a ruler of the synagogue, he would be expected to look askance at Christ's public work, but, in his emergency, he did not let this hinder him. He went straight to Jesus to say that his twelve-year-old daughter was at the point of death, asking Jesus to come and restore her to health. This he believed was possible.

Christ went to the house of the religious leader, in no wise deterred either by a healing on the way or by the report that the visit was hopeless because the girl had already died. The importance of this visit, in Christ's own eyes, is indicated by the fact He allowed only three of the Twelve to accompany Him to the leader's house. These three, Peter, James, and John, clearly constituted an inner circle, the core of the fellowship. It was the same three who went with Him later to the Mount of Transfiguration. Apparently, He felt the need on this occasion of undoubted loyalty and support, as well as counsel. In our concentration on the way that men needed Christ, we sometimes forget the degree to which Christ needed men.

The occasion was important, not merely because of the value of the life of the young girl, but also because of the growing tension with the religious hierarchy. If Jairus might be truly won, what might not follow with other leaders? The whole question of strategy in the growth of a redemptive movement was involved. The contact with the daughter of the household did not come in the midst of a crowd, for the crowd was an obvious handicap. The contact came with a truly select company, namely, the child's parents and the three of the inner circle on whom Christ depended so greatly.

By quieting the unfounded fears, and by speaking as one of the reverent little company, directly to the girl, Christ brought the incident to a fortunate ending. As He truly sensed, the girl was not dead, but only asleep, and the pressure of His hand as well as His affectionate command, aroused her. His primary concern being for the person, Christ asked that the girl be given something to eat. Christ's clear insistence that the news not be spread is an important feature of the total gospel. His attitude was the precise opposite of the desire for publicity which seems to be part of some religious activities. In short, the needy individuals, whom Christ helped, were invariably treated as ends in themselves, rather than as means to His own advancement. Healing arose from human compassion, not from a desire for personal prestige.

16

The Watershed

He went away from there and came to his own country; and his disciples followed him. And on the sabbath he began to teach in the synagogue; and many who heard him were astonished, saying, "Where did this man get all this? What is the wisdom given to him? What mighty works are wrought by his hands! Is not this the carpenter, the son of Mary and brother of James and Joses and Judas and Simon, and are not his sisters here with us?" And they took offense at him. And Jesus said to them, "A prophet is not without honor, except in his own country, and among his own kin, and in his own house." And he could do no mighty work there, except that he laid his hands upon a few sick people and healed them. And he marveled because of their unbelief.

And he went about among the villages teaching.

And he called to him the twelve, and began to send them out two by two, and gave them authority over the unclean spirits. He charged them to take nothing for their journey except a staff; no bread, no bag, no money in their belts; but to wear sandals and not put on two tunics. And he said to them, "Where you enter a house, stay there until you leave the place. And if any place will not receive you and they refuse to hear you, when you leave, shake off the dust that is on your feet for a testimony against them." So they went out and preached that men should repent. And they cast out many demons, and anointed with oil many that were sick and healed them. (6:1–13)

The story of Christ's ministry is marked by a great change immediately after the intense teaching of the Twelve and the individual healings. At that time Christ went to His home territory and, on the Sabbath, entered the synagogue which He had attended so long, and there taught. That He went to the synagogue is not surprising, for He had done that before, after the start of His public work; what is surprising is that this visit was apparently His last one to *any* synagogue. We cannot know that He never entered a synagogue again, but we do know that Mark, in his effort to give a faithful account, mentions no subsequent visit of this nature. That the last reference to attendance at a synagogue should come so early in the story is a highly significant feature of the story.

The most reasonable explanation of this striking change in His effort to reach the Jewish people is that Christ became convinced that the synagogue approach could not succeed. There is no escape from the fact that the visit to the Nazareth synagogue was essentially a failure. The people who listened were intensely critical. How, they reasoned, could He feel so important? They had known Him all his life as a neighbor and had watched His work as a carpenter. They recognized Him as one of a large local family, being well acquainted with His mother's other children, both male and female.

Certainly they thought of Him as part of an ordinary home. How, then, could He be esteemed a mighty prophet? The sad outcome of all this hostility and contempt was that Christ's powers to do good were markedly limited. The pathetic sentence is: "And he could do no mighty work there, except that he laid his hands upon a few sick people and healed them." In short, great as Christ's power was, it was limited in effect by lack of human co-operation and friendly response.

This sad failure became the occasion of a remarkable advance, so that it may accurately be termed a watershed in the strategy of Christ. Convinced that little of value could occur in following conventional ways, Christ determined to multiply His resources by sending out the Apostles. The Twelve had already been selected and partly trained, but heretofore they had not gone out as Christ's ambassadors. The task was so great, and the discouragements of conventional religion so numerous, that a new way, utterly different, had to be tried. Like John, Christ had long had *disciples,* but those who went out two by two were more than disciples. They were emissaries. Out of the defeat at Nazareth came the inauguration of the Christian offensive.

17

The Tragedy of John the Baptist

King Herod heard of it; for Jesus' name had become known. Some said, "John the baptizer has been raised from the dead; that is why these powers are at work in him." But others said, "It is Elijah." And others said, "It is a prophet, like one of the prophets of old." But when Herod heard of it he said, "John, whom I beheaded, has been raised." For Herod had sent and seized John, and bound him in prison for the sake of Herodias, his brother Philip's wife; because he had married her. For John said to Herod, "It is not lawful for you to have your brother's wife." And Herodias had a grudge against him, and wanted to kill him. But she could not, for Herod feared John, knowing that he was a righteous and holy man, and kept him safe. When he heard him, he was much perplexed; and yet he heard him gladly. But an opportunity came when Herod on his birthday gave a banquet for his courtiers and officers and the leading men of Galilee. For when Herodias' daughter came in and danced, she pleased Herod and his guests; and the king said to the girl, "Ask me for whatever you wish, and I will grant it." And he vowed to her, "Whatever you ask me, I will give you, even half of my kingdom." And she went out, and said to her mother, "What shall I ask?" And she said, "The head of John the baptizer." And she came in immediately with haste to the king, and asked, saying, "I want you to give me at once the head of John the Baptist on a platter." And the king was exceedingly sorry; but because of his oaths and his guests he did not want to break his word to her. And immediately the king sent a soldier of the guard and gave orders to bring his head. He went and beheaded him in the prison, and brought his head on a platter, and gave it to the girl; and the girl gave it to her mother. When his disciples heard of it, they came and took his body, and laid it in a tomb. (6:14–29)

The inauguration of the offensive, of which the sending out of the Apostles was the striking signal, was bound to arouse new opposition. Among those who heard of it was Herod Antipas (4 B.C.-A.D. 39) the son of Herod the Great and the Roman tetrarch. He was crafty and luxurious like his father, at once a Jew and an agent of the Roman power. Naturally Antipas feared Christ, as he had feared John the Baptist, because both represented a clear rebuke to his kind of life. His superstitious fear, exaggerated by his bad conscience, made Herod wonder if John had risen.

John had been arrested by Herod because John's stern preaching of moral austerity challenged the semi-incestuous life of the court. The tetrarch had taken to wife Herodias, the former wife of his brother, whose daughter, his niece, was named Salome. Since the life of these people was as immoral and unrestrained as we have come to expect the life of petty dictators to be, it is not surprising that John had no real chance for justice, but was killed in response to a woman's whim. John the

Baptist was a martyr because he had the courage to speak out boldly against corruption in places of power.

The life of John the Baptist was more influential in the career of Christ than it appears superficially to be. John was indeed the forerunner of the gospel, but he was far more than that. Many of the fears and antagonisms which John aroused were transferred to Christ. John's tragic death clearly foreshadowed, in Christ's consciousness, His own tragedy of the cross. His experience showed that, while naked selfish power may not win in the long run, it can win in the short run. The consequent suffering on the part of the innocent is terrible.

John's failure accentuated the need of a new conception of how Christ's Kingdom could be made to endure. Though John had some disciples, it was easy to see that disciples are not enough for the real survival of a movement. What is required, and what John apparently did not have, is a tightly knit group of deeply dedicated men who are conscious of sharing in an ongoing fellowship. Accordingly Christ could say that, in spite of John's greatness, the least in the Kingdom is greater than John. The witness of John was necessary, but it was not sufficient.

18

Compassion on the Hungry Crowd

The apostles returned to Jesus, and told him all that they had done and taught. And he said to them, "Come away by yourselves to a lonely place, and rest a while." For many were coming and going and they had no leisure even to eat. And they went away in the boat to a lonely place by themselves. Now many saw them going, and knew them, and they ran there on foot from all the towns, and got there ahead of them. As he landed he saw a great throng, and he had compassion on them, because they were like sheep without a shepherd; and he began to teach them many things. And when it grew late, his disciples came to him and said, "This is a lonely place, and the hour is now late; send them away, to go into the country and villages round about and buy themselves something to eat." But he answered them, "You give them something to eat." And they said to him, "Shall we go and buy two hundred denarii worth of bread, and give it to them to eat?" And he said to them, "How many loaves have you? Go and see." And when they had found out, they said, "Five, and two fish." Then he commanded them all to sit down by companies upon the green grass. So they sat down in groups, by hundreds and by fifties. And taking the five loaves and the two fish he looked up to heaven, and blessed, and broke the loaves, and gave them to the disciples to set before the people; and he divided the two fish among them all. And they all ate and were satisfied. And they took up twelve baskets full of broken pieces and of the fish. And those who ate the loaves were five thousand men. (6:30–44)

It is a great mistake to think of the gospel as purely spiritual in its nature. There are spiritual religions, but Christianity is not one of them. Throughout Christian history there has been concern for bodies as well as souls. There has been almost as much emphasis upon hospitals as upon places of worship, and the feeding of the hungry, including those formerly known as enemies, has been a marked feature of the modern Christian age. This effort to minister to the whole man, rather than merely to his spiritual needs, does not represent a departure from the Christian genius, but is deeply rooted in the original gospel. The feeding of the five thousand is one of the original demonstrations of this phase of the gospel.

We cannot but be struck by the efforts of Christ and those who, after the inauguration of the new strategy, are called "apostles," to find some time for themselves, but we are equally struck by their failure to achieve the needed privacy. Christ asked the members of the self-conscious fellowship to come apart and rest awhile, but, as soon as they gathered for the required retreat, they were again besieged by the crowds of people, who were able to find them, even in seclusion. What follows is a conflict of two valid requirements, that of the few for rest and that of the many for inspiration and for bread.

Christ's compassion upon the crowd was accentuated

by His recognition of their leaderless condition. Obviously a movement could not be built on them as they were. That is why the provision of trained emissaries was increasingly urgent. Christ knew that He could not address all the crowds and, in any case, He could not address them for long. Each additional day showed the necessity of producing a band of workers in the human harvest field before it was too late.

The scene as it developed in the wilderness is an ideal reminder of the twofold character of the gospel. The harassed and helpless people needed ideas for their minds, but they also needed material food for their bodies. Though the Twelve did not seem to be as much concerned with the latter as with the former, Christ's subsequent action was a rebuke and a lesson to them. The story, as it was told, was a miracle of sharing. By God's grace the meager supplies proved to be more than enough. Whether the event really advanced the Cause of Christ is, however, highly doubtful. There is no evidence that any of the multitude became serious and dedicated followers of Christ. The story, accordingly, involves an element of sadness.

19

Answer to the Terrified

Immediately he made his disciples get into the boat and go before him to the other side, to Bethsaida, while he dismissed the crowd. And after he had taken leave of them, he went into the hills to pray. And when evening came, the boat was out on the sea, and he was alone on the land. And he saw that they were distressed in rowing, for the wind was against them. And about the fourth watch of the night he came to them, walking on the sea. He meant to pass by them, but when they saw him walking on the sea they thought it was a ghost, and cried out; for they all saw him, and were terrified. But immediately he spoke to them and said, "Take heart, it is I; have no fear." And he got into the boat with them and the wind ceased. And they were utterly astounded, for they did not understand about the loaves, but their hearts were hardened.

And when they had crossed over, they came to land at Gennesaret, and moored to the shore. And when they got out of the boat, immediately the people recognized him, and ran about the whole neighborhood and began to bring sick people on their pallets to any place where they heard he was. And wherever he came, in villages, cities, or country, they laid the sick in the market places, and besought him that they might touch even the fringe of his garment; and as many as touched it were made well. (6:45–56)

Again, at Christ's insistence, the inner band journeyed across the Lake of Genessaret. As they needed to get away from the people, so Christ needed to get away from *them*. Accordingly He went alone up a mountainside to pray. The fact that even Christ could not subsist without the repeated experience of solitude tells us something significant about our own lives. No life is good enough without frequent times of being alone. We need to get away from people, not because we do not love them, but because our love is not sufficiently effective, when we *are* with them, if we are *always* with them.

From His elevation on the land, Christ, in the evening, was able to see the hard predicament of His little band, as they rowed fruitlessly against the wind. In the night, His time of prayer over, Christ joined the party while they were evidently still close to shore, having made no real headway up to that time. Even after the striking evidence of Christ's power in the instance of feeding the multitude, His closest followers were still unprepared for His complete control over the forces of nature. Accordingly, they could hardly believe it when, on His joining them, the wind that had so long foiled their best efforts suddenly ceased. They could not yet really believe that Jesus was Lord.

The rhythm between retirement and service, which we have come to expect, and which is integral to Christianity, was further illustrated as the party reached the opposite shore. By this time the reputation of Christ as a healer had spread so thoroughly that the first word of His arrival caused people to bring the sick to Him on litters. Again the numbers were great and the consequent drain on Christ's powers of compassion was correspondingly great.

Important as the act of healing was, we must see it as a diversion from the main task, and almost as a temptation. Christ could have concentrated on healing all of the rest of the available time, and thus avoided the worst enmity of the established leaders, but this activity, valuable as it was to distraught individuals, would have had no enduring effect. The only hope of an enduring effect lay in greater and greater concentration on the redemptive group on the one hand, with eventual challenge of the establishment on the other, in the hope that the miraculous influence of the former would outlive the tragedy of the latter. It may be noted that not one of the mighty acts recorded so far was done with the intention of providing a spectacle at which men would wonder. Each act, relating either to nature or to human nature, was done for a reason. The miracles, far from being breaks with world order, were demonstrations of the basic order, the order of God's loving will.

20

The Danger of Tradition

Now when the Pharisees gathered together to him, with some of the scribes, who had come from Jerusalem, they saw that some of his disciples ate with hands defiled, that is, unwashed. (For the Pharisees, and all the Jews, do not eat unless they wash their hands, observing the tradition of the elders; and when they come from the market place, they do not eat unless they purify themselves; and there are many other traditions which they observe, the washing of cups and pots and vessels of bronze.) And the Pharisees and the scribes asked him, "Why do your disciples not live according to the tradition of the elders, but eat with hands defiled?" And he said to them, "Well did Isaiah prophesy of you hypocrites, as it is written,

'This people honors me with their lips,
    but their heart is far from me;
in vain do they worship me,
    teaching as doctrines the precepts of men.'

You leave the commandment of God, and hold fast the tradition of men."

And he said to them, "You have a fine way of rejecting the commandment of God, in order to keep your tradition! For Moses said, 'Honor your father and your mother'; and, 'He who speaks evil of father or mother, let him surely die'; but you say, 'If a man tells his father or his mother, What you would have gained from me is Corban' (that is, given to God)—then you no longer permit him to do anything for his father or mother, thus making void the word of God through your tradition which you hand on. And many such things you do." (7:1–13)

Not only Herod, as the secular leader, but the religious leaders from Jerusalem began to get wind that something more than a passing challenge of established authority was in process. Accordingly, the Pharisees of Jerusalem journeyed to the Galilean area to see for themselves. They apparently had heard that the new Healer was openly antagonistic to the restrictions which served so vividly to separate Jews from Gentiles. Obvious means of showing the distinction were seen in rigorous observance of the Sabbath rest, in the rejection of certain foods, and in ceremonial washings. The washings were instituted to avoid religious defilement, whenever contact with legally unclean objects had been involved in the necessary undertakings of daily life and commerce. Ceremonial distinction was urgently important to the Pharisees. Separateness had, it seemed to them, been their price of survival as a people, and they were determined not to let it be lost now. They challenged Jesus directly, not because of any laxness on His own part, but because of the reported ceremonial laxness of His followers, which was clearly the consequence of His revolutionary teaching.

The bold challenge of the Pharisees gave Christ a wonderful chance to deal with first principles, so far as vital religion is concerned. What He said was that it is not enough for God to be honored by using some particular linguistic or ceremonial formula. Anyone could do that, and he could, furthermore, do it with no change of heart whatever. He went on to point out that all ceremonies are man-made. Men make the cups, and they make the rules about the handling of cups. Real religion has nothing to do with how cups are washed, but wholly with a new heart and a consequent new life. Christ sounded the note of the great prophets, who had asserted that God does not require burnt offerings or incense, which are easy to produce, but a pure heart which, by contrast, comes with intense difficulty. This approach was especially effective against the Pharisees because they thought of themselves as the inheritors of the prophetic tradition.

Christ showed that tradition, being wholly man's doing, is never sufficient for true religion. It may not be based on intrinsic moral law at all. Indeed it is possible, by manipulating tradition, to subvert or to tone down a moral demand. Far from being apologetic or defensive, Christ immediately took the offensive and attacked the position of His adversaries. By this act He ruled out the possibility of compromise or appeasement. The issue was sharper than the Pharisees had expected it to be.

21

Reality in Religion

And he called the people to him again, and said to them, "Hear me, all of you, and understand: there is nothing outside a man which by going into him can defile him; but the things which come out of a man are what defile him." And when he had entered the house, and left the people, his disciples asked him about the parable. And he said to them, "Then are you also without understanding? Do you not see that whatever goes into a man from outside cannot defile him, since it enters, not his heart but his stomach, and so passes on?" (Thus he declared all foods clean.) And he said, "What comes out of a man is what defiles a man. For from within, out of the heart of man, come evil thoughts, fornication, theft, murder, adultery, coveting, wickedness, deceit, licentiousness, envy, slander, pride, foolishness. All these evil things come from within, and they defile a man." (7:14–23)

Religion can be many things. It may be centered in superstitious practices or in formal observances or in meticulous attention to ethical rules. But all of these, Jesus implied, are far from the reality. The chief way in which Christ made this clear, to the great surprise of those who heard Him, was by the sharpest contrast between the inner and the outer aspects of faith. The essence of His position is that what touches us externally cannot make any real difference, while our inner motives and affections make all the difference that there is.

Externals, as interpreted by Christ, include any kind of physical ceremony, whether laying on of hands, or application of water, or circumcision. He does not say these are evil. His point is that, if a person has the inner reality, none of these is necessary, while if he does not have the reality, none of these will suffice. Circumcision, as the Apostle Paul saw later, is not what counts, but neither does *lack* of circumcision count. The person who avoids the externals of religion needs, therefore, to be made aware of the subtle danger of supposing that there is some extra virtue or spiritual strength in his merely negative position. The life of Christ appears in us, not when we observe ceremonies, and not when we refuse to observe ceremonies, but when each of us becomes "a new creation" (Gal. 6:15).

In applying His incisive principle Christ obviously referred, in part, to the practice of eating only ceremonially clean food. Dietary laws have a big part in a number of religions, including some branches of the Christian faith. Since there is a valid sense in which touching the stomach is essentially the same as touching the skin, Christ interpreted the external as including the alimentary canal. Touching the skin and touching the stomach are both purely physical operations, and both are of passing significance. Neither action reaches the center of man's true being.

All that is evil and all that is good comes from the intangible yet absolutely real center of man's nature. Sin exists as thought or motive or desire or covetousness before it becomes overt fact. The generous deed likewise arises from the generous heart. A man is defiled, not by what someone does to him or fails to do to him, but by the impurity of his basic motives. A man is essentially harmed neither by eating meat nor by failing to eat meat, but by the lack of genuine, unselfish love in his inmost self. There is only one thing of prime importance in true religion and that is the new life of kinship with God which leads to love of His other children.

This clear distinction, which Jesus made, is not likely to impress us sufficiently, because we have heard it often, but it is still needed in the modern world. Though contemporary Christians do not tend to place emphasis upon the rite of circumcision or on ceremonial treatment of foods or utensils, they find other ways of glorifying the incidental. Real blasphemy comes not chiefly by profaning the holy; it comes far more by deifying the essentially trivial.

22

Humor and Courtesy

And from there he arose and went away to the region
of Tyre and Sidon. And he entered a house, and would
not have any one know it; yet he could not be hid. But
immediately a woman, whose little daughter was possessed by an unclean spirit, heard of him, and came and
fell down at his feet. Now the woman was a Greek, a
Syrophoenician by birth. And she begged him to cast the
demon out of her daughter. And he said to her, "Let the
children first be fed, for it is not right to take the children's bread and throw it to the dogs." But she answered
him, "Yes, Lord; yet even the dogs under the table eat
the children's crumbs." And he said to her, "For this saying you may go your way; the demon has left your
daughter." And she went home, and found the child lying
in bed, and the demon gone.

Then he returned from the region of Tyre, and went
through Sidon to the Sea of Galilee, through the region
of the Decapolis. And they brought to him a man who
was deaf and had an impediment in his speech; and they
besought him to lay his hand upon him. And taking him
aside from the multitude privately, he put his fingers
into his ears, and he spat and touched his tongue; and
looking up to heaven, he sighed, and said to him, "Eph-
phatha," that is, "Be opened." And his ears were opened,

his tongue was released, and he spoke plainly. And he charged them to tell no one; but the more he charged them, the more zealously they proclaimed it. And they were astonished beyond measure, saying, "He has done all things well; he even makes the deaf hear and the dumb speak." (7:24–37)

Many of the persons with whom Christ had revealing experiences were persons whose names we do not know. They were otherwise inconspicuous people and usually unfortunate people, but Christ took them seriously. Two of these were inhabitants of Gentile districts, to which Jesus had temporarily retired, presumably because of the growing menace of His enemies. Though the woman and the man in the stories are nameless, they tell us something about Jesus which we might not know so well apart from His experiences with them.

The Greek woman of the story was sorrowful because of her deranged daughter. The woman broke in upon Christ's much needed privacy to seek His help for her unfortunate child. Christ's recorded answer is, on the surface, very difficult for us, because it seems cruel and any kind of cruelty is entirely inconsistent with the remainder of the gospel. His words sound cruel because He is reported as saying that He must feed the children first, that is, His fellow Jews, and not throw bread to dogs, which means Gentiles. There could be no possible justification for the harshness of this remark, if taken literally, and, in any case, He had already healed the demoniac of Gadara who was in Gentile territory. Only one possible explanation remains: Jesus was speaking in a humorous and bantering vein. He was joking, as we joke about the race problem, sometimes as a way of trying to solve it. The hypothesis that Christ's remark was intended to be humorous is supported by the woman's clearly humorous and bantering reply. She might, she said, be a dog, but dogs could have *crumbs*. She didn't ask for much. Christ loved her banter and healed her daughter. It is good to know that our Lord could laugh, and could appreciate a clever rejoinder.

The succeeding story of the deaf man brings out another subtle phase of Christ's character. This person, who was brought to Jesus as He went through the region of the Ten Towns, was obviously suffering from extreme nervousness. The impediment in his speech showed that. The surrounding crowd evidently made his condition worse, even though the people were solicitous for his welfare. Sensing the situation, Christ took the sufferer away from the crowd to heal him privately. Herein lay a revealing sense of courtesy. Instead of making an exhibition of the man, in order to enhance Christ's own prestige as a healer, He saved the man's feelings. Christ's interest was in the unfortunate person rather than in the effect upon the populace. This story is unique to Mark's gospel and we are grateful for it because it makes us able to speak of the courtesy of Jesus.

23

Feeding on Gentile Soil

In those days, when again a great crowd had gathered, and they had nothing to eat, he called his disciples to him, and said to them, "I have compassion on the crowd, because they have been with me now three days, and have nothing to eat; and if I send them away hungry to their homes, they will faint on the way; and some of them have come a long way." And his disciples answered him, "How can one feed these men with bread here in the desert?" And he asked them, "How many loaves have you?" They said, "Seven." And he commanded the crowd to sit down on the ground; and he took the seven loaves, and having given thanks he broke them and gave them to his disciples to set before the people; and they set them before the crowd. And they had a few small fish; and having blessed them, he commanded that these also should be set before them. And they ate, and were satisfied; and they took up the broken pieces left over, seven baskets full. And there were about four thousand people. And he sent them away; and immediately he got into the boat with his disciples, and went to the district of Dalmanutha.

The Pharisees came and began to argue with him, seeking from him a sign from heaven, to test him. And he sighed deeply in his spirit, and said, "Why does this generation seek a sign? Truly, I say to you, no sign shall be given to this generation." And he left them, and getting into the boat again he departed to the other side. (8:1–13)

It is genuinely surprising to find in the gospel narrative two stories of feeding a multitude. The two accounts, this one and the one in Chapter 18 above, are remarkably similar. In the earlier story the number fed is given as five thousand, while, in the present account, the number is four thousand. The earlier story is placed in Jewish territory, while the later one takes place on Gentile soil. The essential similarity of the two accounts has led many scholars to suppose that we have been given two variants of the same event, different locations and times being developed in oral transmission. There is some reason to believe that Luke was the first scholar to reach this conclusion, inasmuch as he did not include the second story of miraculous feeding in his gospel. Mark, however, was convinced that two such events occurred and so told both. Possibly he was eager to show that Christ was as sympathetic to Gentile as to Jewish hunger. The humorous encounter with the Syrophoenician woman is thus given a wholly serious application.

As Jesus returned closer to the familiar territory of His earlier public ministry, a delegation of Pharisees again approached Him. We must remember that they were serious men, genuinely troubled by what Jesus was doing. Undoubtedly they were sincere. In fact, if their position was correct, they had no alternative except to fight Him. On their premises, He was dangerous because

He was deliberately breaking down the wall of separation. If He should succeed, Judaism, as they valued it, would be extinct.

The delegation asked Christ for a "sign." Perhaps He was the long expected Messiah, the revelation of the Father. The fact that they could not let Him alone showed that they had some misgivings about their own resistance to Him. "Are you He that should come, or look we for another?" was the question. What kind of sign or "evidence" they expected is hard to know. If healing and feeding were not enough to convince them, what would suffice?

The fact that Jesus is represented as having groaned in His spirit, indicates that He recognized a complete barrier of understanding. Possibly what the Pharisees wanted was an exhibition of worldly power of the precise kind that He had consciously rejected alone in the wilderness temptation. Perhaps they wanted Him to leap off a pinnacle of the temple and demonstrate God's favor by landing unhurt. But such an exhibition would have been unworthy, because it would have involved the employment of power for its own sake, without any reference to human sorrow and need.

24

The Dual Dangers of the Christian

Now they had forgotten to bring bread; and they had only one loaf with them in the boat. And he cautioned them, saying, "Take heed, beware of the leaven of the Pharisees and the leaven of Herod." And they discussed it with one another, saying, "We have no bread." And being aware of it, Jesus said to them, "Why do you discuss the fact that you have no bread? Do you not yet perceive or understand? Are your hearts hardened? Having eyes do you not see, and having ears do you not hear? And do you not remember? When I broke the five loaves for the five thousand, how many baskets full of broken pieces did you take up?" They said to him, "Twelve." "And the seven for the four thousand, how many baskets full of broken pieces did you take up?" And they said to him, "Seven." And he said to them, "Do you not yet understand?"

And they came to Bethsaida. And some people brought to him a blind man, and begged him to touch him. And he took the blind man by the hand, and led him out of the village; and when he had spit on his eyes and laid his hands upon him, he asked him, "Do you see anything?" And he looked up and said, "I see men; but they look like trees, walking." Then again he laid his hands upon his eyes; and he looked intently and was restored, and saw everything clearly. And he sent him away to his home, saying, "Do not even enter the village." (8:14–26)

Life would often be relatively simple if we could recognize a single danger and concentrate all of our energies on avoiding or counteracting it. It is not especially hard to fight on only one front. But life is seldom that simple. Usually we find that we must avoid errors in more than one direction, for there are many ways of going wrong. The alternative to a recognized evil is not necessarily a good; it may be, and often is, another evil. Our situation is not really improved if, in our effort to avoid the errors of the left, we become enmeshed in the errors of the right.

Such considerations shed light on Christ's pithy saying about the two heresies which He faced, the Pharisaic and the Herodian. To succumb to one while avoiding the other would be no acceptable solution of the problem. Therefore the Christian must be continually aware of dangers on both sides. The dangers are insidious because systems of ideas are like leaven which can grow and multiply, whether they be helpful or harmful. Leaven is not necessarily good. The Twelve were slow to catch the metaphorical meaning of leaven, thinking that Christ was referring to physical bread. His answer was that physical bread is a simple problem compared to that of dealing with the infectious movement of ideas and convictions.

The choice before men seemed to be narrowed to two, that of a vulgar secularism, on the one hand, and that of a narrow self-righteous religion on the other. If these had been the only choices, if they had exhausted the possibilities, the consequent predicament would have been terrible indeed. The clear and immensely significant teaching of Christ is that we are not reduced to such a choice, because there is a third way which is a live option for men. A great deal of the gospel is an effort to show what the nature of this third way is. Christ showed something of the nature of a third alternative in His approach to the blind man of Bethsaida. As in the case of the deaf man, mentioned in Chapter 22, Christ showed his sense of courtesy to the unfortunate person by taking his hand and leading him out of the town, away from the populace, in order to perform the healing. Genuine human kindness may not be the whole of the third way which we seek, but it is a powerful beginning.

The point of the double danger is not merely historical but highly contemporary. In philosophy there are those who would try to force us into either materialism or superstition; in economics, the pressures are to the extreme left and the extreme right. It is important to be as keenly aware of the dangers of a narrow religion as of the dangers of unbelief. Both may be arrogant in tone and, in fact, remarkably similar. To escape a pagan totalitarianism by accepting a religious totalitarianism does not solve the problem at all.

25

The Recognition of Christ

And Jesus went on with his disciples, to the villages of
Caesarea Philippi; and on the way he asked his disciples,
"Who do men say that I am?" And they told him, "John
the Baptist; and others say, Elijah; and others one of the
prophets." And he asked them, "But who do you say that
I am?" Peter answered him, "You are the Christ." And he
charged them to tell no one about him.

And he began to teach them that the Son of man must
suffer many things, and be rejected by the elders and the
chief priests and the scribes, and be killed, and after
three days rise again. And he said this plainly. And Peter
took him, and began to rebuke him. But turning and seeing his disciples, he rebuked Peter, and said, "Get behind me, Satan! For you are not on the side of God, but
of men."

And he called to him the multitude with his disciples,
and said to them, "If any man would come after me, let
him deny himself and take up his cross and follow me.
For whoever would save his life will lose it; and whoever
loses his life for my sake and the gospel's will save it.
For what does it profit a man, to gain the whole world
and forfeit his life? For what can a man give in return
for his life? For whoever is ashamed of me and of my
words in this adulterous and sinful generation, of him

73

will the Son of man also be ashamed, when he comes in the glory of his Father with the holy angels." And he said to them, "Truly, I say to you, there are some standing here who will not taste death before they see the kingdom of God come with power." (8:27–9:1)

Jesus kept the secret of who He was for a long time and He even kept it from those whom He had recruited as trusted helpers. Finally the truth became known, but it was not known until Jesus put the question of His identity directly. It was not sufficient for the disciples to repeat what others might say in explaining His identity; they were asked what their own conviction was. Suddenly, as by inspiration, there came to one of the men, the fisherman named Simon, the stupendous realization that Jesus was, in reality, the long expected Messiah. To know how bold this conclusion was we need to remember how slightly Jesus resembled the popular picture of what a Messiah would be. Simon's conclusion seemed to contradict nearly all of the available evidence.

The conviction which came to the simple fisherman at Caesarea-Philippi is that which stands at the heart of all the Christian creeds. The earliest creed is the little phrase, "Jesus is Lord." What this means is at once both very simple and very profound. Every sincere Christian is trying, however inadequately, to say that Jesus is "the Express Image" of the Father. If we would know what God is, it is not enough to set our eyes upon the mountains or the stars or even the laws of nature, so brilliantly revealed in contemporary science; we must, instead, set our eyes upon *Jesus*. God, we believe, is, in eternity,

74

what Jesus was in time. This is what we mean by calling Him Christ and not merely Jesus. In short, Christians, ever since the day spent near the upper reaches of the Jordan, have recognized that God is like Jesus. God has *been,* even before the creation of the world, but usually He has been known imperfectly. In Jesus, we have come to know God's face.

Once the recognition of the tremendous fact was made, it was necessary for Christ to engage in urgent teaching, designed to correct false expectations. He had to show them that, in one sense, He was *not* the Christ they had confidently expected. Peter could make the initial leap of recognition, but he could not, at first, bear the revelation that the Express Image of the Father would be marked by suffering and humility, rather than by conquering power. Worldly power may be a barrier rather than a genuine revelation. The whole conception of what success is must be turned upside down. The new redemptive life of Christ's surprising Kingdom need not be reserved for the long future; it can be a present reality.

26

Withdrawal on the Mountain

And after six days Jesus took with him Peter and James
and John, and led them up a high mountain apart by
themselves; and he was transfigured before them, and
his garments became glistening, intensely white, as no
fuller on earth could bleach them. And there appeared
to them Elijah with Moses; and they were talking to
Jesus. And Peter said to Jesus, "Master, it is well that we
are here; let us make three booths, one for you and one
for Moses and one for Elijah." For he did not know what
to say, for they were exceedingly afraid. And a cloud
overshadowed them, and a voice came out of the cloud,
"This is my beloved Son; listen to him." And suddenly
looking around they no longer saw any one with them
but Jesus only.

And as they were coming down the mountain, he
charged them to tell no one what they had seen, until the
Son of man should have risen from the dead. So they kept
the matter to themselves, questioning what the rising
from the dead meant. And they asked him, "Why do the
scribes say that first Elijah must come?" And he said to
them, "Elijah does come first to restore all things; and
how is it written of the Son of man, that he should suffer
many things and be treated with contempt? But I tell
you that Elijah has come, and they did to him whatever
they pleased, as it is written of him." (9:2–13)

Though the rhythm of withdrawal and encounter is exhibited at many points in the gospel narrative, it is exhibited most vividly in reference to the experience on the Mount of Transfiguration. After the tremendously moving experience of recognition, and the first real effort to revolutionize men's expectations about the Messiah, Christ needed to be away. This time He needed to be with a few of His closest associates, rather than entirely alone. He had learned that the best way to escape the pressures of the crowd was to go up into the heights. The factual character of this particular withdrawal is indicated by the definiteness of the dating; it was "after six days."

On the mountain the three men of the inner circle, Peter, James, and John, joining with Jesus in meditation and prayer, saw everything in a new light, because they understood at last that their Teacher was not merely a teacher. In moments of ecstasy they saw vividly the whole unfolding story of the giving of the law and the work of the prophets, both of which pointed beyond themselves to a needed completion. The overwhelming conclusion was that the completion had at last come, and that the whole movement of Israel's history was thereby fulfilled.

The climax of the religious experience on the mountain, so far as the members of the inner circle were concerned, was the immediate sense of God's presence and the divine assertion that Jesus was, indeed, His Beloved Son. Here was a corroboration of the insight at Caesarea-Philippi. First Simon had sensed that Jesus was the

Christ, then Jesus Himself had verified the judgment, and now finally there came the verification from God the Father that Jesus was His Express Image.

Though the central conviction was now clear, and though the direct religious experience on the mountain was indubitable, the three were still puzzled about how to connect their revolutionary insight with the conventional teaching of the scholars concerning the way in which the Messiah was to come. How about the forerunner, Elias? In answer, Christ returned to that most exciting of tenses, the completed present. As the Authorized Version translates it, He said, "But I say unto you, that Elias indeed is come." This completed and immediate present is still the major tense of the Christian faith. Once the Mount of Transfiguration was for three fishermen; now it is for all who will make the climb.

The chief way in which we can discover whether the basic teachings of the gospel are really true or merely imaginary is to participate in the ongoing fellowship of verification. The probability of truth increases as this fellowship is enlarged through the centuries.

27

Encounter on the Plain

And when they came to the disciples, they saw a great crowd about them, and scribes arguing with them. And immediately all the crowd, when they saw him, were greatly amazed, and ran up to him and greeted him. And he asked them, "What are you discussing with them?" And one of the crowd answered him, "Teacher, I brought my son to you, for he has a dumb spirit; and wherever it seizes him, it dashes him down; and he foams and grinds his teeth and becomes rigid; and I asked your disciples to cast it out, and they were not able." And he answered them, "O faithless generation, how long am I to be with you? How long am I to bear with you? Bring him to me." And they brought the boy to him; and when the spirit saw him, immediately it convulsed the boy, and he fell on the ground and rolled about, foaming at the mouth. And Jesus asked his father, "How long has he had this?" And he said, "From childhood. And it has often cast him into the fire and into the water, to destroy him; but if you can do anything, have pity on us and help us." And Jesus said to him, "If you can! All things are possible to him who believes." Immediately the father of the child cried out and said, "I believe; help my unbelief!" And when Jesus saw that a crowd came running together, he rebuked the unclean spirit, saying to it, "You dumb and deaf spirit, I command you, come out of him, and never enter him again." And after crying out and convulsing him terribly, it came out, and the boy was like a corpse; so that most of them said, "He is dead." But Jesus took him by the hand and lifted him up, and he arose. And when he had entered the house, his disciples asked him privately, "Why could we not cast it out?" And he said to them, "This kind cannot be driven out by anything but prayer." (9:14–29)

When Jesus and the Three went up into the mountain for their retreat, most of the disciples remained below on the plain and continued to meet with the people. The assemblage included both the scribes who were the critics of Christ and the unfortunate people who sought help either for themselves or for their loved ones. As soon as Christ came down the mountain He was plunged right back into the confusion of controversy and need. The temptation to stay on the mountain must have been great, because on the mountain there was peace and a sense of direct communion with the Father, but it is wrong to stay always on the mountain as it is wrong to stay always on the plain. Service to needy people is more helpful if it is broken by retirement, and retirement is more productive if it leads straight back to the difficulties of ordinary experience in the world.

The most shocking fact about Christ's retirement for spiritual renewal is the fact that, by engaging in retirement, He was actually seeming to neglect, for the time at least, human miseries He could have relieved. He stayed on the mountain, apart from the people, at the very time that they were clamoring for help. This we know because they were there waiting on His return to them, and because the disciples had already tried to help, but were not able to do so. This is part of the toughness of Christ's character, which we sometimes find it convenient to forget. He cared so much that He had to have times apart, if His caring was to be sufficiently effective. The duty to be alone is as much a religious duty as is the duty to serve.

The point of this emphasis on the price of effective service is shown in Christ's answer to the perplexed question of His followers who could not understand the reason for their own failure to heal the demoniac boy. They were delightedly surprised at Christ's sudden and opportune return to them, but they were genuinely puzzled at the fact that they could not succeed in healing as He did. The answer Christ gives is the simple one that they have not paid a sufficient price in personal devotion. He was genuinely shocked at their ineptitude and at their basic misunderstanding of their own situation. His remark indicates something of how lonely He felt. The ability of the disciples to understand Him seemed to lessen rather than grow with the passing days.

28

A Revolution in Values

They went on from there and passed through Galilee.
And he would not have any one know it; for he was
teaching his disciples, saying to them, "The Son of man
will be delivered into the hands of men, and they will
kill him; and when he is killed, after three days he will
rise." But they did not understand the saying, and they
were afraid to ask him.

And they came to Capernaum; and when he was in the
house he asked them, "What were you discussing on the
way?" But they were silent; for on the way they had discussed with one another who was the greatest. And he
sat down and called the twelve; and he said to them,
"If any one would be first, he must be last of all and
servant of all." And he took a child, and put him in the
midst of them; and taking him in his arms, he said to
them, "Whoever receives one such child in my name receives me; and whoever receives me, receives not me but
him who sent me."

John said to him, "Teacher, we saw a man casting out
demons in your name, and we forbade him, because he
was not following us." But Jesus said, "Do not forbid him;
for no one who does a mighty work in my name will be
able soon after to speak evil of me. For he that is not
against us is for us. For truly, I say to you, whoever gives

you a cup of water to drink because you bear the name of Christ, will by no means lose his reward. (9:30–41)

After the drama of the mountain and the plain, the movements of Christ and His close followers became even more secret. It was abundantly clear that tragedy lay ahead and that the time to prepare the little fellowship for their ordeal was very short. Now He became explicit about His impending death, which was the logical outcome of the enmity He had aroused. Either the religious or the secular authorities or a combination of both had to kill Him. His attacks on what they stood for were so fundamental that He really left them no other way, short of accepting His lordship.

The almost unbelievable depths of the misunderstanding on the part of his followers is shown by their arguments about prestige and power. He had tried deliberately and repeatedly to tell them that His Kingdom would be marked by suffering and that, far from engaging in struggles for precedence, those who really followed Him would be humble servants, but it appears that almost nothing of this reached them. They had ears, but they did not hear, because their own presuppositions deafened them.

Recognizing, without their saying so, that the disciples had argued among themselves about who would be leaders when the Kingdom should be established, Christ called the Twelve to one side at Capernaum and sought to make His revolutionary teaching about the real values of human life even more explicit. The ideal, He said, is exactly the opposite of what the people of the world, whether secular or ecclesiastic, seek. In order to achieve the clarity inherent in an acted parable, He called their attention visibly to a little child in His arms. In the world men pride themselves on prudential wisdom, but the purpose of a Christian is to be a child. The child spirit is a goal and not merely a starting point. Though not all children demonstrate it, the ideal child spirit is of one who seeks to learn, because he knows that he does not know, and of one who trusts his parent unreservedly. At best, the world of a child is a world of wonder, unspoiled by cynical judgment of others or by the corrosive effect of consciously hidden motives. The end, says Christ, is to rediscover the beginning.

The disciples were not only envious of potential leadership on the part of their companions; they were also jealous of others who might try to have some real part in Christ's movement. Some saw a chance to get ahead and they wanted to limit the competition as strictly as possible. This is the point of the reference to another, not of the inner group, who was accomplishing Christian healing. Christ's answer is the answer to all Christian exclusiveness in any age. No person has a monopoly on the redemptive fellowship. If anyone really helps, do not attack him, says Christ, merely because he seems to be an outsider. We are not so rich in resources that we can disdain any.

29

Salting with Fire

"Whoever causes one of these little ones who believe in me to sin, it would better for him if a great millstone were hung around his neck and he were thrown into the sea. And if your hand causes you to sin, cut it off; it is better for you to enter life maimed than with two hands to go to hell, to the unquenchable fire. And if your foot causes you to sin, cut it off; it is better for you to enter life lame than with two feet to be thrown into hell. And if your eye causes you to sin, pluck it out; it is better for you to enter the kingdom of God with one eye than with two eyes to be thrown into hell, where their worm does not die, and the fire is not quenched. For every one will be salted with fire. Salt is good; but if the salt has lost its saltness, how will you season it? Have salt in yourselves, and be at peace with one another."

And he left there and went to the region of Judea and beyond the Jordan, and crowds gathered to him again; and again, as his custom was, he taught them. (9:42–10:1)

The complement to Christ's liberalism concerning welcome to outsiders who render genuine service is His sternness concerning the condemnation of insiders who are lacking in tenderness. Just as anyone who renders the least service to a follower of Christ is to be counted within the circle of blessing, whatever he may call himself, anyone who claims to be within the circle and is insensitive to human need is a heretic at heart. The real divisions, in short, are not the divisions which normally appear.

The demands upon the Christian are far harder than the disciples suppose. The Christian life is presented by Christ, not as the sentimental belief in natural goodness, but as a hard and dangerous road, which involves both severe temptations and continual dangers. It may be necessary to endure sacrifices in order to avoid fatal temptations. Though the love of God, as Christ has shown elsewhere, is always available, His emphasis here is upon the dangerous character of the path which every Christian is called upon to travel. Life, especially for the Christian, is not one of easy choices, but often a school of struggle, in which some things have to be given up if others are to be obtained. So great is the issue that, by making wrong choices, the loss to the individual may be eternal rather than merely temporal. Small temporal losses are as nothing when seen in the context of eternity.

The reference to salt, which comes at the climax of this passage, is similar to that placed by Matthew at a crucial point in the Sermon on the Mount (Matt. 5:13), but Mark adds two sentences which are unique to his account. The first is the remark that everyone will be salted with fire, a violent figure of speech which may refer to persecution. If so, it is presented as universal and normal for Christ's followers. If the little group, unworthy as its members are, is destined to preserve the world, as salt preserves meat, we have here the added notion that such salt is not really effective in its holy task except as it is refined by suffering. Thus the grim note continues. Not all that appears to be saving salt is really so, but may be mere dirt, with the genuine salt washed out of it.

The second unique Marcan sentence is "Have salt in yourselves, and be at peace with one another." Here is an unforgettable paradoxical statement of the double nature of the Christian demand. We must be both tough and tender; we must be hard with ourselves while we are generous in our estimates of others; we must engage in a constant inner fight at the same time that we try to be peaceful; we must be more ready to endure suffering than we are to inflict it.

We have reason to be grateful to Mark for including his statement about salt and peace, because the paradox thus indicated is inherent in the whole life of a Christian. It is easy to be peaceful, if we do not stand for principle, because then we simply appease the aggressor and let him have his way, though that way may bring great harm to mankind. On the other hand, it is relatively easy to have the strong salt of principle, standing resolutely for justice, providing we have no responsibility also to keep the peace. A Christian is one who must always hold in tension these two ideals.

30

The Home in the Kingdom

And Pharisees came up and in order to test him asked, "Is it lawful for a man to divorce his wife?" He answered them, "What did Moses command you?" They said, "Moses allowed a man to write a certificate of divorce, and to put her away." But Jesus said to them, "For your hardness of heart he wrote you this commandment. But from the beginning of creation, 'God made them male and female.' 'For this reason a man shall leave his father and mother and be joined to his wife, and the two shall become one.' So they are no longer two but one. What therefore God has joined together, let not man put asunder."

And in the house the disciples asked him again about this matter. And he said to them, "Whoever divorces his wife and marries another, commits adultery against her; and if she divorces her husband and marries another, she commits adultery."

And they were bringing children to him, that he might touch them; and the disciples rebuked them. But when Jesus saw it he was indignant, and said to them, "Let the children come to me, do not hinder them; for to such belongs the kingdom of God. Truly, I say to you, whoever does not receive the kingdom of God like a child shall not enter it." And he took them in his arms and blessed them, laying his hands upon them. (10:2–16)

The question about divorce which Christ's enemies propounded, was evidently intended to place Him in a dilemma. If He stood for easy divorce, He came into conflict with the Jewish law, while if He condemned divorce, His judgment could be brought to the attention of Herod who might do to Christ what he had already done to John the Baptist when that prophet spoke out boldly on this touchy theme.

Christ's way of dealing with the problem was to transcend the role of the rule maker by reaching down to deeper principles which underlie the whole concept of the home. Thus He avoided both the leaven of the Pharisees and the leaven of Herod. To this end He pointed out that the Mosaic reference to divorce (Deut. 24:1-4) is not a positive moral judgment but a recognition of a problem. It is a reaction to failure rather than a positive moral counsel. He went further in connection with Moses by referring to the more profound statement of the divine purpose of marriage found in Genesis 1:27.

What Christ did was to lift the problem of marriage out of its legalistic context and to present it as part of the divine order. The home is not an easy subject for legal manipulation, as weights and measures might be, for the home is truly a foretaste of the Kingdom. The family represents a commitment rather than a contract; it is personal identification. To emphasize this, Christ quoted the passage, about husband and wife becoming one, which He knew so well from Genesis 2:24.

In lifting up this high spiritual ideal of marriage Christ did not answer the captious question of His critics. The passage does not establish the absolute indissolubility of marriage. Matthew, in his account of the same incident, makes an exception in the case of unchastity (Matt. 19:9). Apparently Jesus recognized the possible justification of divorce, but He chose, in this encounter, to place His emphasis on the positive conception of the home as a holy place. The blessing of the little children at once emphasizes the Christian scale of values and also indicates the further significance of the home. A home is a place where children belong and that is part of the reason for its potential holiness. The church is not the only form of the Christian society; the home is intended to be an equally redemptive fellowship.

Christianity is perverted whenever it is presented as a meticulous system of who can be married by the church and who cannot. That is the leaven of the Pharisees, quite as evil as is the looseness, which represents the leaven of Herod. What Christ does, instead, is to glorify and dignify family life. Therefore a sincere understanding Christian can never teach that celibacy is intrinsically better or more truly righteous than married life is. The home, like the church, is meant to be a Christian society.

31

Significance of Riches

And as he was setting out on his journey, a man ran up and knelt before him, and asked him, "Good Teacher, what must I do to inherit eternal life?" And Jesus said to him, "Why do you call me good? No one is good but God alone. You know the commandments: 'Do not kill, Do not commit adultery, Do not steal, Do not bear false witness, Do not defraud, Honor your father and mother.'" And he said to him, "Teacher, all these I have observed from my youth." And Jesus looking upon him loved him, and said to him, "You lack one thing; go, sell what you have, and give to the poor, and you will have treasure in heaven; and come, follow me." At that saying his countenance fell, and he went away sorrowful; for he had great possessions.

And Jesus looked around and said to his disciples, "How hard it will be for those who have riches to enter the kingdom of God!" And the disciples were amazed at his words. But Jesus said to them again, "Children, how hard it is to enter the kingdom of God! It is easier for a camel to go through the eye of a needle than for a rich man to enter the kingdom of God." And they were exceedingly astonished, and said to him, "Then who can be saved?" Jesus looked at them and said, "With men it is impossible, but not with God; for all things are possible with God." (10:17–27)

Christ's reaction to the rich young ruler demonstrates equally His humility, His affection, and His realism. Though He was the express image of God, He distinguished between Himself and God, not only, as we have seen above, by engaging in the act of prayer, but also, now, by refusal to attribute to Himself the complete goodness which belongs to God. In view of who He was, and what He could do, our Lord's humility is nothing short of amazing.

We can be glad that we have the specific reference to the fact that Christ loved the young man. This seeker was not merely one of a succession of cases interviewed by Jesus. The relationship quickly became personal, partly, we suppose, because Christ admired the man's forthright answer about the commandments. But Christ, though affectionate, was also realistic enough to know that something was wrong. He saw that the man was hindered by caring too much about the wrong thing, namely, his possessions. Love rules life, but sometimes the loves are in mutual conflict. The young man's love of wealth was a challenge and a barrier to his love of God. Jesus appealed to him, accordingly, to make a revolutionary change in his life, by giving up his wealth entirely, but this radical step the man was unwilling to take. The story, therefore, is fundamentally a sad story.

Christ was not condemning the use and possession of money. He could not do so, because the elimination of all ownership would undermine ordered society. Giving is a virtue, but people cannot give unless they *have*. What Christ taught was that any finite object of love becomes evil when it is wholly dominant. Since a little change means almost nothing, the barrier must, sometimes, be removed completely. If the particular man in question had given up half of his wealth, nothing of a redemptive nature would have been accomplished. Sometimes, unless the dose for a sick man is a big dose, it is the same as nothing at all.

Christ does not make the command a universal one, and He does not say that it is impossible for a rich man to enter into the kingdom of God. Instead, He says that it is difficult. Part of the difficulty arises from the sense of security, with lack of need, which often marks the man of wealth. Security is itself a barrier to spiritual growth. The broken and the needy are far closer to the Kingdom than are those who feel adequate and successful. God reaches us most easily when there is a crack in our armor. The barriers of our own making, which effectively exclude us from the Kingdom, are real and in some cases almost insurmountable, but with God all is possible.

32

Cost of Discipleship

Peter began to say to him, "Lo, we have left everything and followed you." Jesus said, "Truly, I say to you, there is no one who has left house or brothers or sisters or mother or father or children or lands, for my sake and for the gospel, who will not receive a hundredfold now in this time, houses and brothers and sisters and mothers and children and lands, with persecutions, and in the age to come eternal life. But many that are first will be last, and the last first."

And they were on the road, going up to Jerusalem, and Jesus was walking ahead of them; and they were amazed, and those who followed were afraid. And taking the twelve again, he began to tell them what was to happen to him, saying, "Behold, we are going up to Jerusalem; and the Son of man will be delivered to the chief priests and the scribes, and they will condemn him to death, and deliver him to the Gentiles; and they will mock him, and spit upon him, and scourge him, and kill him; and after three days he will rise." (10:28–34)

It is clear that Christ never allowed any of His followers to suppose that participation in His cause, if it were genuine, would be easy. He could, indeed, say that

His yoke was easy, that is, that it was perfectly fitted, and that His burden was correspondingly light, but He never said that the burden was or would be eliminated. The burden was carried bravely and even gaily, but it was always a burden, even to the end.

The Apostles were men who often misunderstood their Teacher's revolutionary message, but in any case they paid a price to become His recruits. Certainly they left their means of livelihood in whole or in part and they had to be away from their familes a great deal. Often they felt the sting of unpopularity and they felt it more strongly as the drama of Christ's earthly life neared its climax.

It is an error to suppose that Christ was never concerned with rewards. He was so concerned and He said that the rewards of fellowship with Him would be great, but they would not be what the followers expected, and certainly they would not be what the world expects. However great the reward may be in other ways, it will include *persecutions*. Accordingly, participation in persecution and abuse is part of the cost of discipleship, without which the fellowship of the redemptive society cannot be shared.

Christ's words as they started to Jerusalem, and therefore to the cross, accentuated the message of renunciation which was given to the rich young man and the prediction of persecution given to the disciples. Ultimate victory and glory were assured, but the road ahead was long and rough and painful. Here is the first really clear indication to the followers of the nature of Christ's suffering and death. It is no wonder that they were amazed, particularly since some, attracted by His infectious presence, had undoubtedly expected worldly preferment with the political rise of the new Leader.

What is bound to move us, as we read Christ's words uttered on the road to Jerusalem, is the detailed accuracy of His prediction. He saw the inevitability of the conflict and the form that it must take. Though we can see this, with the advantage of coming after the event, the Apostles, living on the other historical side of the cross, could not have had the same reaction. They seem to have been overawed by the strange resolution of their Master, but, because they loved Him, they followed without understanding.

Christianity gives much to its adherents, but it is always perverted when it is presented as a success story. The gospel may do a great many things for us, but it is deeply misunderstood if it is interpreted merely as a psychological instrument for our help. It is, instead, a relationship which begins with a dangerous and uncalculating commitment.

33

Transvaluation of Worldly Values

And James and John, the sons of Zebedee, came forward to him, and said to him, "Teacher, we want you to do for us whatever we ask of you." And he said to them, "What do you want me to do for you?" And they said to him, "Grant us to sit, one at your right hand and one at your left, in your glory." But Jesus said to them, "You do not know what you are asking. Are you able to drink the cup that I drink, or to be baptized with the baptism with which I am baptized?" And they said to him, "We are able." And Jesus said to them, "The cup that I drink you will drink; and with the baptism with which I am baptized, you will be baptized; but to sit at my right hand or at my left is not mine to grant, but it is for those for whom it has been prepared." And when the ten heard it, they began to be indignant at James and John. And Jesus called them to him and said to them, "You know that those who are supposed to rule over the Gentiles lord it over them, and their great men exercise authority over them. But it shall not be among you; but whoever would be great among you must be your servant, and whoever would be first among you must be slave of all. For the Son of man also came not to be served but to serve, and to give his life as a ransom for many." (10:35–45)

The clearest evidence of the extreme degree of the Apostles' misunderstanding of Christ is the request of the sons of Zebedee. What they asked was special preferment when positions of authority should be allocated. It was as though, in a political campaign, two of the party workers should try to arrange with the candidate for cabinet posts in the event of the success of the party at the polls.

If this request had come from some of the men who operated on the fringes of the movement, it would not have been so surprising, but it was genuinely shocking when it came, not merely from members of the Twelve, but from members of the Three. It is almost incredible that this self-seeking request could come from men who had joined Jesus on the Mount of Transfiguration.

The value of this story is that it gives Christ His very best opportunity to try to make us understand the truly revolutionary nature of the Christian fellowship. It is hard for us to realize this today because so much of the subsequent Christianity has obscured the sharp contrast. The church, itself, has often refused the baptism with which Christ was baptized, in that it has reflected worldly standards of prestige and wealth and power.

In Christ's pronouncement there is the sharpest contrast between His way and the way of the world. The worldly way is perfectly understandable; it is the way in which men try to get ahead, receive laudatory honors, and attain positions of authority over other men. The worldly way is to try to secure appointments to positions, not only for the service which can thereby be rendered, but also for the personal sense of superiority which the appointment gives. Men love to be ecclesiastics, partly because they can wear gorgeous vestments and because they are frequently addressed by flattering titles. All this bears far more resemblance to a worldly court than to the radical humility which was enjoined by Christ. Men love to be called "Doctor," thus being singled out from the masses for a special recognition. Indeed, such practices are accepted so generally that we tend to forget that Christ warned specifically against them. Christ, in His conception of a moral order, sought to turn the world upside down, and this He did by saying that the goal is not to be a ruler; the goal is to be a servant.

One of the saddest aspects of Christian history is seen in the way in which the church so soon forgot Christ's teaching about humility, and began, within a few centuries, to demonstrate many of the characteristics of the Roman Empire, which it partly replaced. Finally it did not seem strange that the very ones who claimed to represent Christ's cause would be called "princes of the church." It is bad enough when the church is unable to change the world; it is worse when the church itself becomes worldly.

34

A New Disciple

And they came to Jericho; and as he was leaving Jericho with his disciples and a great multitude, Bartimaeus, a blind beggar, the son of Timaeus, was sitting by the roadside. And when he heard that it was Jesus of Nazareth, he began to cry out and say, "Jesus, Son of David, have mercy on me!" And many rebuked him, telling him to be silent; but he cried out all the more, "Son of David, have mercy on me!" And Jesus stopped and said, "Call him." And they called the blind man, saying to him, "Take heart; rise, he is calling you." And throwing off his mantle he sprang up and came to Jesus. And Jesus said to him, "What do you want me to do for you?" And the blind man said to him, "Master, let me receive my sight." And Jesus said to him, "Go your way; your faith has made you well." And immediately he received his sight and followed him on the way. (10:46–52)

The story of the blind man of Jericho who was relieved of his blindness is one of the slightest stories of the gospel. Indeed, it is so slight that we may wonder at its inclusion in the gospel narrative. Nevertheless, all three of the Synoptic Gospels include the incident and they include it in approximately the same form, except that in Matthew's account Bartimaeus has a blind companion with him, who is also healed.

If the poor man, living on the edge of ancient Jericho, had been told that his name would be remembered and used hundreds of years later and in distant lands, he would have been incredulous. But this incredible development has occurred and it has occurred because, modest as he was, his modest life was associated once with the life of Christ. Since there must have been many examples of healing on the slow journey to Jerusalem, why was the Jericho incident selected for remembrance? This we do not wholly know, but there are at least three features which make the story unique or nearly so.

The first element of uniqueness lies in the blind man's boldness in addressing Christ as "Son of David," a title which Jesus did not reject. The time had come, it seems, to throw off secrecy and to enter Jerusalem as the real Messiah, though one who challenged popular expectations. The blind man's language thus anticipated both the triumphal entry and the words placed over the cross, "The King of the Jews." We cannot understand Christ if we fail to see that He thought of Himself as King, even though He rejected utterly the kind of kingship represented by the Caesars or Herods.

The fact that the blind man of Jericho addressed the One he could not see as "Son of David," which is to say "The Messiah," is highly suggestive. It is not reasonable that the stranger would know anything of the detailed ancestry of Jesus. The most reasonable conclusion is that the rumor was spreading, by word of mouth, that Jesus really was the Anointed One whom they expected. The blind man was undoubtedly aware of the considerable crowd going by and of what its members were saying to one another. The spread of such a rumor would explain Pilate's reaction to Jesus when their famous encounter took place.

A second point which makes the story stand out is seen in the fact that Christ went out of His way to call the man. He did not let the beggar make all the approach, but asked His companions to call the man. Reflecting the nature of the Father, Christ searched for men, even more than they searched for Him. The blind man's faith was immensely strengthened when he realized that, humble as he was, he was being sought.

The third part of the story which is memorable is the blind man's response. After receiving his sight, the man was set free by Jesus to go his way, but, instead of going about his business, he followed Christ on the road to Calvary. In this case, Christ allowed the discipleship to occur, instead of ordering the man to stay home and make his witness there. The situation was changed; extra followers were welcomed; the assumption of kingship was near.

35

Entry into Jerusalem

And when they drew near to Jerusalem, to Bethphage and Bethany, at the Mount of Olives, he sent two of his disciples, and said to them, "Go into the village opposite you, and immediately as you enter it you will find a colt tied, on which no one has ever sat; untie it and bring it. If any one says to you, 'Why are you doing this?' say, 'The Lord has need of it and will send it back here immediately.'" And they went away, and found a colt tied at the door out in the open street; and they untied it. And those who stood there said to them, "What are you doing, untying the colt?" And they told them what Jesus had said; and they let them go. And they brought the colt to Jesus, and threw their garments on it; and he sat upon it. And many spread their garments on the road, and others spread leafy branches which they had cut from the fields. And those who went before and those who followed cried out, "Hosanna! Blessed be he who comes in the name of the Lord! Blessed be the kingdom of our father David that is coming! Hosanna in the highest!"

And he entered Jerusalem, and went into the temple; and when he had looked round at everything, as it was already late, he went out to Bethany with the twelve. (11:1–11)

If we face the last days of Christ before the crucifixion with a conscious attempt to free our minds of presuppositions we are struck by the evidences that Christ's cause had some of the features of an underground movement. One of the evidences is the arrangement about the colt which was to play such an important part in the triumphal entry. What is obvious is that there had been previous planning and that some members of the movement were already operating in the vicinity of Jerusalem. The colt was deliberately tied in a prearranged location and a password had been established in case of difficulty. Actually the local co-operators did demand the certainty that those who came for the colt were the proper ones and, the right phrase having been used, they allowed the colt to go.

Here we have the marks of a partially secret movement emerging into public gaze. This gives the act of entry tremendous significance. Though Christ and His followers could undoubtedly have entered Jerusalem in relative secrecy, it is clear that He determined to adopt the strategy of open challenge of the authorities. Going on in partial secrecy would not have accomplished what needed to be accomplished. In order to draw attention to this phase of the gospel the followers of Christ, with His compliance, put on something of an exhibition. The event has the marks of having been carefully planned rather than being entirely spontaneous.

Here the new public feature is the open acceptance of kingship. It is still different from worldly kingship, because there are no soldiers or war horses in the parade, and because Christ rides on a lowly animal, but royalty is what is publicly affirmed. The deliberate connection with the kingship of David is explicitly recorded. Christ's boldness must have been as disconcerting to the authorities as was His radical transvaluation of what kingship involves.

Though the hard core of Christ's loyal followers determined the character of the public demonstration, they were evidently joined by others, including Galilean pilgrims who were coming to Jerusalem for the Passover festival. Each, then, hailed what he thought he saw. Some hailed the now famous Healer; others hailed the uncrowned King, God's long expected Representative.

Much about the triumphal entry is hard for us to understand. If Christ was making an announcement, why did He not make it more clearly? Why did He allow the people to speak, but did not speak Himself? The steps from absolute secrecy, to partial publicity, to the full publicity of the cross seem painfully slow. The constant feature was the presentation of truth in such a fashion that those who were ready would be able to discern it.

36

The Impatience of Christ

On the following day, when they came from Bethany, he was hungry. And seeing in the distance a fig tree in leaf, he went to see if he could find anything on it. When he came to it, he found nothing but leaves, for it was not the season for figs. And he said to it, "May no one ever eat fruit from you again." And his disciples heard it. And they came to Jerusalem. And he entered the temple and began to drive out those who sold and those who bought in the temple, and he overturned the tables of the moneychangers and the seats of those who sold pigeons; and he would not allow any one to carry anything through the temple. And he taught, and said to them, "Is it not written, 'My house shall be called a house of prayer for all the nations'? But you have made it a den of robbers." And the chief priests and the scribes heard it and sought a way to destroy him; for they feared him, because all the multitude was astonished at his teaching. (11:12–18)

The character of Christ had many facets. That He was both tough and tender, with one feature sometimes uppermost in appearance and sometimes the other, is obvious. Though He was tender with the blind men and recognized sinners, He was exceedingly hard with the self-righteous. The hard side of His character comes out vividly as soon as the decision is made to present to the authorities an open challenge.

The first evidence of Christ's stern mood is found in the acted parable of the Divine Impatience. He uses the illustration of the fruitless fig tree, by which He clearly means the Jewish faith, to point out that sometimes patience ceases to be a virtue. The reference to the fruitless tree, which is too brief in Mark's account to be readily understandable, is clarified by the story in Luke 13:6–9. In this fuller story of divine impatience the verdict is that the tree which has been given every chance, and even an extra year of grace, and yet is fruitless, should be cut down. It is better, sometimes, to plant a new tree than to waste time and energy on one that is worn out. This observation reflects Christ's personal judgment on the old order. It had had its chance and deserved to be replaced. Further patience would be a vice.

The vivid impatience of Christ was soon demonstrated by what He did in the temple. It seemed to Him that the intended use of this great structure had been almost entirely perverted. A religion, He realized, can be so altered in practice that it finally defeats its original purpose, even though the same words are kept. This had occurred in the Jerusalem temple, which had been built as a means of facilitating the sense of reverence. Now the reverent atmosphere was dissipated because religion had become a business and a highly profitable one. All that He had taught about the danger of riches and the search for riches seemed to be illustrated here, in the very place where it should have been avoided. The immediate reaction of Christ was one of holy anger. So great was His moral indignation that, although He was without auxiliaries, the people who were engaged in the religious business quailed before Him. That He employed physical force is shown by His overturning tables and chairs. In short, Christ threw down the gauntlet. He had attacked the enemy in its citadel and henceforth the struggle was even more bitter.

We understand better the boldness of Christ's act in the temple when we recognize the probability that this deed, more than any other, brought about His death. It is important to notice that, as a result of Christ's dramatic temple attack, with its fierce impatience of the prostitution of faith, the chief priests and scribes were afraid of Him. They saw all the worldly and religious security which they had built so carefully, suddenly endangered. It was in jeopardy because of the fierce courage of one person and the admiration which He engendered among the people.

37

Unlimited Faith

And when evening came they went out of the city. As they passed by in the morning, they saw the fig tree withered away to its roots. And Peter remembered and said to him, "Master, look! The fig tree which you cursed has withered." And Jesus answered them, "Have faith in God. Truly, I say to you, whoever says to this mountain, 'Be taken up and cast into the sea,' and does not doubt in his heart, but believes that what he says will come to pass, it will be done for him. Therefore I tell you, whatever you ask in prayer, believe that you receive it, and you will. And whenever you stand praying, forgive, if you have anything against any one; so that your Father also who is in heaven may forgive you your trespasses." (11:19–26)

Being always the Teacher, whatever else He was, Christ took time, even after His entry into the Jerusalem arena, to continue the training of the group on whose perseverance the future of the movement depended. Sometimes He taught by what He did not say, as well as by what He said. Thus, when Peter referred to Christ as having "cursed" the unfruitful tree, Jesus, as though further explanation were itself fruitless, changed the subject and turned Peter's attention to the affirmative conception of faith in God.

The potency of faith, as interpreted by Jesus, is something which it is almost impossible to exaggerate. He went out of His way to affirm that, by prayer, the apparently impossible could be accomplished. The extreme illustration He used referred to the very mountain on which the city stood, which, He said, could be removed into the sea by the prayer of a person of sufficient faith.

It is clear that Christ was not inhibited, as we tend to be, by being overimpressed with the supposed limitation imposed by natural law. Many of us find it impossible, with intellectual integrity, to believe in physical miracles, but, when the situation is analyzed, it appears that our only reason for disbelief is the simple conviction that natural law is immutable. Though we do not mean to be irreverent in our position, the truth is that we are thereby, in our philosophy, putting something which God has made above God Himself. Without fully realizing the absurdity, we are putting the creature above the Creator. Often we are really not believing in God at all, except as some remote First Cause, for we are actually putting our faith in what is substantially an impersonal or mechanical order. If the order of the universe is a mechanical order, it is obvious that miracles do not occur and we may as well cease to discuss prayer or providence, but the notion that the order is mechanical is by no means self-evident.

Though Christ never had to face our contemporary temptation to think of natural law as an autonomous system, independent of the Purposive order in God's love and care, it is not difficult to see what His answer would have been. He saw God the Father as the Maker and Sustainer of the entire world, One to whom men could pray and One to whom *He* prayed. God, being the God of all the universe or universes, giving meaning to the whole by His infinite purpose, was Lord of all, and was therefore Lord of natural law. Law, in such an understanding, is not something with an independent existence, but only our name for the general dependability of the divine purpose. The limitation on the power of prayer is not natural law; it is the lack of forgiveness on the part of the one who prays.

This emphasis on forgiveness as the condition of fully effective prayer is a matter of prime importance. It reminds us, near the end, of the lesson involved in the early story of the paralytic. The difference is that, whereas the paralytic needed to be forgiven, the first requirement of most men who pray is that they be *forgiving*. Lingering bitterness or nursing of a sense of personal injustice can be a genuine barrier to the fully religious life, which is the life of prayer. The combination of forgiving others and being forgiven is the same that is involved in the Lord's Prayer.

38

The Basis of Authority

And they came again to Jerusalem. And as he was
walking in the temple, the chief priests and the scribes
and the elders came to him, and they said to him, "By
what authority are you doing these things, or who gave
you this authority to do them?" Jesus said to them, "I
will ask you a question; answer me, and I will tell you by
what authority I do these things. Was the baptism of
John from heaven or from men? Answer me." And they
argued with one another, "If we say, 'From heaven,' he
will say, 'Why then did you not believe him?' But shall
we say, 'From men'?"—they were afraid of the people,
for all held that John was a real prophet. So they answered Jesus, "We do not know." And Jesus said to them,
"Neither will I tell you by what authority I do these
things." (11:27–33)

Once Christ had appeared openly with royal claims on
His entrance into the city, and particularly after His vehement attack on vested interests in the temple, it was
inevitable that His enemies would become even more
outspoken in their criticism. Accordingly, when He returned to the cleansed temple, the leading religious
authorities, of various orders, joined to attack Him. Their

point of attack was Christ's lack of authority for what seemed to them to be highhanded acts. Conceivably there were abuses in the temple, after the accretion of years, and conceivably these abuses ought to be ended, but who gave Him, they wanted to know, the authority to engage in the act of reformation? In essence, they asked Him what committee He represented.

As might be expected, Jesus countered the attack by taking the offensive. He was not the first, He reminded them, to take things into His own hands when situations had become intolerable. John the Baptist had done the same by his unauthorized preaching of national repentance. The very essence of the vocation of a prophet is that he listens to the voice of God more than to the voices of men. What, Christ wanted to know, was John's basis of authority? The question was more than clever; it was profound, for it went to the root of the matter. The reason the enemies of Jesus could not tell what the human authorization of John's preaching had been was that there *was* none.

In the ordinary course of events a human system of authority is a good thing. In the management of a business or an institution, it is impossible to operate if individuals down the line make unauthorized purchases and allocate funds in an irregular manner. If a business is not conducted methodically it soon ceases to be a business at all. But, however true this may be of the affairs of ordinary life, the time comes when, in connection with the greatest issues, it does not apply at all. Sometimes the system of religious authority becomes so hardened that

113

the crust has to be broken by a powerful thrust from beneath. If Amos had waited for some authorization of his preaching, he would have waited forever and in vain. Entrenched privilege, whether civil or ecclesiastic, does not arrange easily for its own destruction. Sometimes the barren tree must be uprooted and the only one with the courage to uproot it is the person who has the boldness which arises from the direct sense of God's leading.

The way in which Jesus, in His answer to the delegation of the Sanhedrin, associated Himself with John the Baptist, is highly revealing. His particular work, of course, was not identical with that of John, but both knew what it was to be divinely commissioned by the Father. Both were sent by God, wholly without any necessity of human mediation, the one to do great deeds and the other to do greater deeds. To ask the authority of one sent from God is to ask a question which, in the nature of things, cannot be answered. There is no authority of the kind that official bodies depend upon, recognize, and grant. The question was fundamentally meaningless because it assumed something contrary to fact.

39

The Parable of the Vineyard

And he began to speak to them in parables. "A man planted a vineyard, and set a hedge around it, and dug a pit for the wine press, and built a tower, and let it out to tenants, and went into another country. When the time came, he sent a servant to the tenants, to get from them some of the fruit of the vineyard. And they took him and beat him, and sent him away empty-handed. Again he sent to them another servant, and they wounded him in the head, and treated him shamefully. And he sent another, and him they killed; and so with many others, some they beat and some they killed. He had still one other, a beloved son; finally he sent him to them, saying, 'They will respect my son.' But those tenants said to one another, 'This is the heir; come, let us kill him, and the inheritance will be ours.' And they took him and killed him, and cast him out of the vineyard. What will the owner of the vineyard do? He will come and destroy the tenants, and give the vineyard to others. Have you not read this scripture:

'The very stone which the builders rejected
has become the head of the corner;
this was the Lord's doing,
and it is marvelous in our eyes'?"

And they tried to arrest him, but feared the multitude,

for they perceived that he had told the parable against them; so they left him and went away. (12:1–12)

The parable of the vineyard is more bitter and violent than most of the parables of Jesus, largely, we infer, because it was spoken directly to His enemies. They understood perfectly that they were some of the characters in the story and the consequence was that they hated Him even more. His strategy seemed to be to force them either to accept Him or to kill Him. He left them no other alternative.

The vivid parable is really an allegory, one in which Christ appears as one of the characters, namely, the Father's own beloved Son. This open avowal of Messianic status is consistent with this entire section of the gospel record, a section in which there is less reticence about the Messiahship than appeared previously. The servants who are sent one after another to give warning, are the prophets, and the husbandmen who will kill not only the prophets, but even the Son, are the members of the religious establishment, represented in the present by the very company of those who are listening so uncomfortably.

The story describes the history of Israel, a history marked by God's choosing a people to demonstrate His purpose, however unworthy they prove to be. In spite of their rejection of His overtures, God sends a succession of prophets, each building on the work of his predecessors and each making a new appeal, but one after another faces rejection or contempt. Finally, in a grand climax of unrequited love, God sends His own Son, His special Messenger, but even He will be killed. Thus Jesus taunts His persecutors with the prediction of what they are about to do. The prediction must have taken away any satisfaction the religious leaders may have felt in their vengeful act. They could not even accuse Him of being wrong in predicting an escape from a tragic end.

The story of the vineyard helps us to see that Christ looked upon Himself as God's final appeal to His people. Consequently their expected rejection would lead to some new development, the planting of a new tree to take the place of the fundamentally barren one that was encumbering the ground. The outcome was to be a new kind of community, far more nearly universal and one with an amazing power to penetrate common life. The parable envisaged the end of one chapter in God's dealing with men and the start of another. The parable was given a striking conclusion by the quotation of part of the 118th Psalm. Because the leaders respected the Scriptures it must have been disconcerting to have these used so brilliantly by their adversary. Hope, Jesus taught, will come in wholly unexpected ways.

40

Limits of Secular Power

And they sent to him some of the Pharisees and some of the Herodians, to entrap him in his talk. And they came and said to him, "Teacher, we know that you are true, and care for no man; for you do not regard the position of men, but truly teach the way of God. Is it lawful to pay taxes to Caesar, or not? Should we pay them, or should we not?" But knowing their hypocrisy, he said to them, "Why put me to the test? Bring me a coin, and let me look at it." And they brought one. And he said to them, "Whose likeness and inscription is this?" They said to him, "Caesar's." Jesus said to them, "Render to Caesar the things that are Caesar's, and to God the things that are God's." And they were amazed at him. (12:13–17)

There is grim irony in the fact that Christ's enemies of both kinds finally consolidated their attack. The two groups hated Him for different reasons, but hatred, when it is strong enough, can produce strange bedfellows. Already Christ had warned against equally dangerous though radically different infections of Pharisaism and Herodism, but now, in Jerusalem, the Pharisees and the Herodians came together to try to embarrass and discountenance Him in the eyes of the people on whom He depended for support.

Then, as now, the dangerous topics were politics and religion, the most dangerous consisting of the union of the two. The question of tribute to Caesar combined the issues of faith and sovereignty in a fashion highly satisfactory to Christ's critics. If He should say that it was lawful to pay tribute, He would affront the fierce nationalism of the common people as well as of the Pharisaic party, while, if He denounced tribute to the imperial power of Rome, he could be in serious trouble so far as the Roman authorities were concerned. It looked as though He would be proven disloyal to *somebody*.

Christ, of course, recognized the question as a trap rather than a serious inquiry. All His noble talk about listening to God rather than to the opinions of men could be undermined, His critics believed, by any answer He might make. They were certainly trying to create a forced option in which two and only two alternatives would exhaust the area of possibility. Since they were being mundane and earthy in their question, He decided to be more earthy still and asked for a minted coin. Using the coin's image of the Emperor as His starting place, Christ refused to deal merely with simple alternatives and carried the question to a deeper level. Their mistake, He implied, was the mistake of oversimplification. It is true that men owe something to the state, but, with no contradiction, they also owe something radically different and far more important to God.

The use of a coin showing the Emperor's likeness has

especial significance in view of the comparative rarity of portraiture of any kind. The opposition to the representation of the human form was deep seated among the Jews, though the faces of the later Herods finally came to adorn some coins.[1] In Christ's time the monetary portraiture of Caesar represented one of the most vivid symbols of the Roman secular power in contrast to the religious heritage of Israel. The coin, therefore, was the perfect starting point for an understanding of the rich principle of multiple allegiance.

The principle of double and limited loyalty which Christ enunciated has borne marvelous fruit in both political theory and political practice. "Those words," wrote Lord Acton in *The History of Freedom in Antiquity*, "gave to the civil power, under the protection of conscience, a sacredness it had never enjoyed and bounds it had never acknowledged: and they were also the repudiation of absolutism and the inauguration of freedom."

[1] Much new light is shed upon the episode by the recent publication, by the Abingdon Press, of two important new books, *The Life and Times of Herod the Great* and *The Later Herods*. Both were published in America in 1958.

41

Resurrection of the Dead

And Sadducees came to him, who say that there is no resurrection; and they asked him a question, saying, "Teacher, Moses wrote for us that if a man's brother dies and leaves a wife, but leaves no child, the man must take the wife, and raise up children for his brother. There were seven brothers; the first took a wife, and when he died left no children; and the second took her, and died, leaving no children; and the third likewise; and the seven left no children. Last of all the woman also died. In the resurrection whose wife will she be? For the seven had her as wife."

Jesus said to them, "Is not this why you are wrong, that you know neither the scripture nor the power of God? For when they rise from the dead, they neither marry nor are given in marriage, but are like angels in heaven. And as for the dead being raised, have you not read in the book of Moses, in the passage about the bush, how God said to him, 'I am the God of Abraham, and the God of Isaac, and the God of Jacob'? He is not God of the dead, but of the living; you are quite wrong." (12:18–27)

The account of Christ's encounter with the Sadducees is one of the best attested of all elements of the gospel record, in that all three of the Synoptic writers give the story in full and all give it in essentially the same way. It is obvious that the teaching inherent in the story seemed important to the early Christians. It is not surprising that it should seem important, for it deals with a question which no thoughtful person can avoid. All of us know that we shall die and we know, furthermore, that those whom we love and value most will also die. We may not be greatly worried about our own destinies, but, when affection is real, we are bound to be concerned with the destiny of others.

The most remarkable feature of Christ's handling of the issue of life after death is that He speaks directly of resurrection and not merely of immortality. Immortality, in the general sense that something survives, might be merely the continuance of influence or it might be the endurance of an impersonal realm of spirit, to which the individual spirit returns as the drop of water returns to the ocean, though it loses its particular identity.

The clear teaching of Christ is that resurrection is a fact. The captious critic, in the person of the supposedly sophisticated Sadducee or any other, raises a number of difficulties. If we are truly resurrected, they ask, will there not be problems of jealousy? Christ's answer in this matter, as in other difficult problems, involves the strategy of carrying the issue to a deeper level. To live again, in all reality, He suggests, does not mean to suffer involvement in all of the limitations of this present inadequate life of suffering and jealousy and pride. Now we have marriage, but it is not necessary to suppose that we shall have marriage then. The resurrected life will be one in which personal identity, which is a thing of unsurpassed value, will be maintained, but one in which the bitterness and inequalities of earthly life will be transcended.

It is not surprising, in view of both Christ's teaching and His personal demonstration, that the Christian creeds have affirmed unequivocally the resurrection of the body. By this is meant some means of individual recognition. We do not understand, of course, exactly what a spiritual body would be, but we do understand its function: it would enable us to know one another. Since what is infinitely valuable in God's eyes is the individual person, some means of individuation must be preserved after the decay of physical bodies. Merely physical bodies will not suffice because they involve so much of disease and inequality of opportunity.

Christ's faith in the life everlasting is clear and unequivocal because it is based directly upon the love of God. If we are indeed God's offspring, His care is bound to extend to the life on the other side of the grave as well as this side. It is really as simple as that.

42

The Paradox of Double Priority

And one of the scribes came up and heard them disputing with one another, and seeing that he answered them well, asked him, "Which commandment is the first of all?" Jesus answered, "The first is, 'Hear, O Israel: The Lord our God, the Lord is one; and you shall love the Lord your God with all your heart, and with all your soul, and with all your mind, and with all your strength.' The second is this, 'You shall love your neighbor as yourself.' There is no other commandment greater than these." And the scribe said to him, "You are right, Teacher; you have truly said that he is one, and there is no other but he; and to love him with all the heart, and with all the understanding, and with all the strength, and to love one's neighbor as oneself, is much more than all whole burnt offerings and sacrifices." And when Jesus saw that he answered wisely, he said to him, "You are not far from the kingdom of God." And after that no one dared to ask him any question. (12:28–34)

Few of the questions which were asked of Christ were such that they could be answered with a simple affirmative or negative. This is not because Christ avoided a direct answer, but because human life is of such a complex nature that the answers to most problems must be compound. This is conspicuously true in the problem of the highest single moral demand. When asked what it is, Jesus could not answer simply, because the truth is that there is no single moral requirement of supreme standing. The ultimate requirements, Christ said, are not one, but *two*. There are, as Matthew suggests, two "firsts" (Matt. 22:39).

The way in which Christ used the Hebrew Scripture to bring together the two supreme obligations fills us with wonder and admiration. The one "first" commandment was exactly what His hearers expected, the Shema (Deut. 6:4) which was repeated daily by the Jews. To love God with all of one's being was, they agreed, the very foundation of monotheism. One striking feature of the formula, as employed by Christ, however, is the subtle way in which He amplified it. Though they differ in the order of the basic words, all three of the Synoptic writers agree that Christ added, "and with all your intellect," a phrase which does not occur in the quoted Hebrew text. The Hebrew of Deuteronomy includes only three of Mark's great words, "heart," and "soul," and "strength." We are bound to suppose that Christ's additional term was intentional and therefore important.

The great significance of Christ's additional term lies in the consequent demand, so far as a Christian is concerned, for intellectual integrity. It is not enough for religion to appeal to imagination and emotion, important as they are. If it leaves out intellect it is not really whole. The Christian must so discipline his mind that he can

125

meet all opposition on its own ground. The task of reason is to rule out automatically all dishonest or merely comforting faith. What the student does in the laboratory may be as much a Christian responsibility as what he does in a prayer meeting.

The other "first," which is of equal standing, is the requirement that a person love his neighbor as himself. Christ drew this statement out of what would seem to be an unlikely place, the book of Leviticus (19:18). Leviticus seems an improbable source because so much of it is a recitation of outworn rules and legalistic formulations, but it may be compared to a slag heap with a priceless jewel imbedded in it. This jewel Christ recognized and saved for all mankind.

There are many different religions in the world, each major one having some real merit, but there can be no adequate faith which does not include Christ's insight about the paradox of double priority. There are, inevitably, two poles to the good life. The love of God is of transcendent importance, but if it is not associated with the practical obligations to our fellow men, it is inevitably self-centered. The cultivation of inner spiritual life without constant social concern constitutes a heresy. On the other hand, the love of one's neighbor, without a grounding in the love of God, easily becomes mere philanthropy and finally is superficial secularism. The only hope lies in involving both priorities in one living context. We must keep the roots and the fruits of our faith together, because they need each other.

43

Professionals and an Amateur

And as Jesus taught in the temple, he said, "How can the scribes say that the Christ is the son of David? David himself, inspired by the Holy Spirit, declared,

'The Lord said to my Lord,
Sit at my right hand,
till I put thy enemies under thy feet.'

David himself calls him Lord; so how is he his son?" And the great throng heard him gladly.

And in his teaching he said, "Beware of the scribes, who like to go about in long robes, and to have salutations in the market places and the best seats in the synagogues and the places of honor at feasts, who devour widows' houses and for a pretense make long prayers. They will receive the greater condemnation."

And he sat down opposite the treasury, and watched the multitude putting money into the treasury. Many rich people put in large sums. And a poor widow came, and put in two copper coins, which make a penny. And he called his disciples to him, and said to them, "Truly, I say to you, this poor widow has put in more than all those who are contributing to the treasury. For they all contributed out of their abundance; but she out of her poverty has put in everything she had, her whole living." (12:35-44)

Increasingly, Christ found it necessary to make clear His deep conflict with the scribes, that is, the professional theologians. He sought to go over their heads to the common people, who were glad to hear such a fresh voice. His effort was to break through the limitations imposed by both scholarship and tradition, in order to find what the coming of Christ could mean. Concern with genealogy reaching back to King David was, for example, trivial, and Jesus sought to lead men beyond trivial matters. The Messiah is more than David's heir; His appeal, consequently, is potentially universal. Though He was of Davidic descent, this did not seem to Christ to be a point of importance.

The lesson which Christ sought to teach about the true nature of religious life is made vividly by the contrast between the professionals and one amateur. The professionals, says Christ, may be far from the Kingdom, even though they use correct and pious words. They love to appear in some kind of religious garb, with the result that they receive from the people both deference and privilege. They sit at the head tables and thus seem to be important people. Their religious profession, then, far from being a matter of personal sacrifice, is a means of self-advancement and a basis of prestige. But, for all the apparent concern for the religious life, it does not keep them from promoting harsh deals, when opportunity offers. They devour widows' houses, perhaps by taking rich fees for performing religious services to individuals.

In the sharpest possible contrast to this arrogant professionalism in religion, Mark tells the story of a rank amateur, a poor widow who, when she visited the temple, made a contribution which was a tiny one, but it was all that she had. Christ observed this scene and was deeply moved by it. In this case He did not need to create a story for a lesson, because here was a true story which had just occurred. Consequently He spoke to His closest followers about the incident in order to make them understand that the action of this religious amateur illustrated His teaching exactly. She did not wear long robes; she did not receive homage from others; but her commitment was real because it was total. Here, then, is what real religion is about. It is not a matter of ceremonies or prestige or hierachies of any kind. Instead, it is the total commitment of loving souls. Giving is to be measured, not by amount, but by proportion.

44

Beyond Optimism and Pessimism

And as he came out of the temple, one of his disciples said to him, "Look, Teacher, what wonderful stones and what wonderful buildings!" And Jesus said to him, "Do you see these great buildings? There will not be left here one stone upon another, that will not be thrown down."

And as he sat on the Mount of Olives opposite the temple, Peter and James and John and Andrew asked him privately, "Tell us, when will this be, and what will be the sign when these things are all to be accomplished?" And Jesus began to say to them, "Take heed that no one leads you astray. Many will come in my name, saying, 'I am he!' and they will lead many astray. And when you hear of wars and rumors of wars, do not be alarmed; this must take place, but the end is not yet. For nation will rise against nation, and kingdom against kingdom; there will be earthquakes in various places, there will be famines; this is but the beginning of the sufferings.

"But take heed to yourselves; for they will deliver you up to councils; and you will be beaten in synagogues; and you will stand before governors and kings for my sake, to bear testimony before them. And the gospel must first be preached to all nations. And when they bring you to trial and deliver you up, do not be anxious beforehand what you are to say; but say whatever is given you in that hour, for it is not you who speak, but the Holy Spirit. And brother will deliver up brother to death, and the father his child, and children will rise against parents and have them put to death; and you will be hated by all for my name's sake. But he who endures to the end will be saved." (13:1–13)

Christ was not an optimist. Though the Kingdom was, in some sense, a potentially present reality, and therefore His teaching was Good News, He understood perfectly the sordidness of the human scene and the deep tragedy of human history. He promised greatness and glory, but He did not promise ease or simple prosperity. Even such an evidence of human success as the great building of the temple failed to impress Him, because He recognized the impermanence of such structures. His insight into the temporary character of this structural glory was verified, in the fall of Jerusalem about forty years later, when, after dreadful slaughter, the temple was destroyed by the soldiers of Titus. It was destroyed, said Tacitus, "to root out the superstition of Jews and Christians."

Christ's really serious consideration regarding future history was given not to the crowd, and not even to the Twelve, but to an inner group of four, the first fishermen followers. These naturally hoped to learn precisely when the great expected climax of history would come, but Jesus did not satisfy them. Instead, He pointed out the immensity of the danger of being led astray on this point. We are reminded of the still more unequivocal statement of Christ recorded in Luke 17:20, when He said, "The kingdom of God is not coming with signs to be observed."

The message about which Christ was most clear was that things will be worse before they are better. Human development is not a simple progress from ignorance to enlightenment and consequent justice for all. This might be possible, were it not for the deep evil in the human heart, which leads to unbelievable cruelty. Christ was no mere pessimist, because He knew the glory that can be revealed here and now, often in inconspicuous lives, like that of the poor widow who gave the two copper coins. He did not speak of total depravity, which would be inconsistent with the great conviction that God has made all men in His image. But likewise Christ was no mere optimist, speaking of the innate goodness of human souls. He knew how bitter, how cruel, and how self-seeking the sons and daughters of earth can be. The horrors of concentration camps may have shocked our generation, but they would not have shocked Him, for He understood the many facets of the human heart. Sufferings are intrinsic to the gospel and every Christian must be personally involved in them.

45

The Untrustworthiness of Forecasters

"But when you see the desolating sacrilege set up where it ought not to be (let the reader understand), then let those who are in Judea flee to the mountains; let him who is on the housetop not go down, nor enter his house, to take anything away; and let him who is in the field not turn back to take his mantle. And alas for those who are with child and for those who give suck in those days! Pray that it may not happen in winter. For in those days there will be such tribulation as has not been from the beginning of the creation which God created until now, and never will be. And if the Lord had not shortened the days, no human being would be saved; but for the sake of the elect, whom he chose, he shortened the days. And then if any one says to you, 'Look, here is the Christ!' or 'Look, there he is!' do not believe it. False Christs and false prophets will arise and show signs and wonders, to lead astray, if possible, the elect. But take heed; I have told you all things beforehand. (13:14–23)

Though there was a sense in which the common people heard Christ gladly, there was another sense in which He alienated them. Whereas the people naturally hoped for a restoration of Jewish national splendor, Christ frankly

133

predicted a terrible debacle, not unlike that predicted earlier by Daniel. We do not know how much Mark's account is colored by later events, coming between Christ's public ministry and the final writing of the book, but it seems perfectly clear that Christ did predict the fall of Jerusalem, that He anticipated disaster and tribulation both for the Jewish nation and for His own followers, and that He warned them against anxiety in the face of trouble.

As Christ considered coming tragedy, He saw it not merely in national, but also in intensely human terms. When real calamity comes, like that of military defeat or violent revolution, His concern is for the individual farmer working in his field, or for the woman who is burdened with either pregnancy or the care of a small child. This interest in the lives of women and their special problems is one of the roots of the Christian teaching which has led so powerfully to the liberation of woman in subsequent generations. There is a special revelation of Christ's tenderness in His prayerful hope that the flight of the refugees should not involve the extra hardship of winter cold. Individual suffering and individual pain were so important to Him that Christ saw historical developments in personal terms.

One of the strongest evidences of Christ's accurate understanding of human nature is His observation that men, including supposedly religious men, would use times of tribulation to foster their own private ends. He saw that some men will always glory in periods of confusion and disaster as they prey upon the natural anxiety of distraught people. Thus each great war brings with it the confident assertion that the current conflict is Armageddon and that the final denouement of history is immediately upon us. Jesus seems to have expected all this and to have warned specifically against it. Far from supposing that the path of the Christian cause would be strewn with roses, Christ said that there would be dangers even from His supposed followers. His effort was to help guard against dangers by means of the clear understanding that such dangers were to be expected.

It is hard to see how any careful student of the gospel can make confident predictions about the end of the age, as is done in every generation. One would suppose that such people would be given serious pause by noting the words of Jesus about the untrustworthiness of such forecasters. The truth is that prediction is not only a risky business but is essentially inconsistent with the teaching of Christ. There may, indeed, be an end to history, and it may come in our time, but, if so, we cannot know it. Therefore the Christian way is to give ourselves as compassionately as possible to the human needs which are immediately present.

46

The Kingdom of the Future

"But in those days, after that tribulation, the sun will be darkened, and the moon will not give its light, and the stars will be falling from heaven, and the powers in the heavens will be shaken. And then they will see the Son of man coming in clouds with great power and glory. And then he will send out the angels, and gather his elect from the four winds, from the ends of the earth to the ends of heaven.

"From the fig tree learn its lesson: as soon as its branch becomes tender and puts forth its leaves, you know that summer is near. So also, when you see these things taking place, you know that he is near, at the very gates. Truly, I say to you, this generation will not pass away before all these things take place. Heaven and earth will pass away, but my words will not pass away.

"But of that day or that hour no one knows, not even the angels in heaven, nor the Son, but only the Father. Take heed, watch; for you do not know when the time will come. It is like a man going on a journey, when he leaves home and puts his servants in charge, each with his work, and commands the doorkeeper to be on the watch. Watch therefore—for you do not know when the master of the house will come, in the evening, or at midnight, or at cockcrow, or in the morning—lest he come suddenly and find you asleep. And what I say to you I say to all: Watch." (13:24–37)

The message about the eventual coming of the Son of Man is one of the most difficult parts of the gospel for us to understand. It must have been difficult for the earliest disciples, but in some ways it is even more difficult for us, because, since we live nearly two thousand years later, we know that the events mentioned have not come to pass. Did Christ expect a sudden shift in the entire course of history within a reasonably short time? If so, He was mistaken, for this has not occurred. We are still muddling along, with many mistakes and some victories, and we have never seen "the Son of man coming in clouds with great power and glory." Perhaps, on the other hand, He was not mistaken, and *we* have mistaken what He meant.

In trying to find a reasonable answer to this problem we must never forget that Christ presented the Kingdom as *both* present and future. It certainly was meant as present when He said (Luke 17:21) "The kingdom of God is in the midst of you." The crucial phrase here may also be understood as "within you." The reign of God was, in one sense, affirmed rather than predicted. But, in another sense, it was clearly of the future, because it is obvious that much of the present course of history is a sinful and willful revolt against the divine order.

Though it is hard for secular-minded modern men to accept it, there is nothing fundamentally unreasonable about a true Second Coming, in which the confusions and failures of our human history are completely redeemed by the sovereign power of the Living God. Certainly we know that man himself cannot bring Utopia, because, even in our best efforts, there is an admixture of human pride, conceit, and struggle for power. If we go on as we are going on now, in a continuous development of historical events, a thousand years from now there will still be men who will sacrifice others to the enhancement of their own prestige. If the kingdom comes fully, therefore, it will have to be God's doing. Herein lies the validity in the idea of the Second Coming.

If this is Christ's point, the postponement for hundreds or even thousands of years is a mere detail, and in no way invalidates the basic conviction. In any case, we can be certain about Christ's emphasis on the impossibility of prediction. Here the crucial passage is that in which He said that even He did not know. This is a rebuke to any person in any generation who *claims* to know. Because no man knows, or can know, humble watchfulness is the only mood that is reasonable.

47

The Grace of Extravagance

It was now two days before the Passover and the feast of Unleavened Bread. And the chief priests and the scribes were seeking how to arrest him by stealth, and kill him; for they said, "Not during the feast, lest there be a tumult of the people."

And while he was at Bethany in the house of Simon the leper, as he sat at table, a woman came with an alabaster jar of ointment of pure nard, very costly, and she broke the jar and poured it over his head. But there were some who said to themselves indignantly, "Why was the ointment thus wasted? For this ointment might have been sold for more than three hundred denarii, and given to the poor." And they reproached her. But Jesus said, "Let her alone; why do you trouble her? She has done a beautiful thing to me. For you always have the poor with you, and whenever you will, you can do good to them; but you will not always have me. She has done what she could; she has anointed my body beforehand for burying. And truly, I say to you, wherever the gospel is preached in the whole world, what she has done will be told in memory of her." (14:1–9)

We can be grateful for the way in which the gospel record moves back and forth between profound teaching and the stories of the lives of simple people. Even with the hostility of the establishment growing more ominous daily, Christ's enemies biding their time in order to strike at the strategic moment and thus avoid the wrath of the people, Christ took time to engage in pleasant fellowship. True to His reputation as one who feasted rather than fasted, He dined with His modest friends, His host at Bethany being a man afflicted with leprosy. We miss the whole point of the scene if we neglect the note of gaiety. An anonymous woman made the party even more gay by anointing Christ's head with a precious liquid.

With a glorious imprudence the woman broke the container at the same time that she seemed to waste its contents. There is a time, her act seemed to say, when people should be careful, but there is also a time when they ought not to be careful. There is something to be said for long saving on necessities in order to make possible a great moment of unrestrained luxury. In such a mood the unknown woman let herself go and helped to demonstrate an important element in Christianity. The Christian is not the one who, with clenched teeth and stern countenance, holds on to the bitter end. Instead, he is one who sings and who, because he knows that God reigns, does not feel that all the weight of the world is on his particular shoulders.

It is important to know that Christianity does not teach moderation. This we know partly by the fact that Christ defended the immoderate act of the woman, and, furthermore, by the absence of the word "moderation" from the New Testament. The word seems to appear in Philippians 4:5, but is not really there, for the word is actually "forbearance," which is another matter altogether. When Professor Whitehead wrote that a certain excessiveness is an ingredient of true greatness, he was writing in conformity with the Christian understanding of human life.

Christ saw that the action of the woman who wasted her precious possession, insignificant as it might seem, was really one of such importance that it would be remembered wherever the gospel would be preached. And this has, indeed, come true. The apparently trivial incident is one which we need. The Christian life is not a meticulous striving for moral perfection; it is a continual prodigality of heart, as we give ourselves to Christ. Prudence is not a Christian virtue though it is undoubtedly a pagan virtue. Christ went out of His way to say that the most important things were hidden from the wise and prudent. The unjust steward was commended by his employer for his prudence, but this does not mean that, in the Christian context, prudence is good. The antithesis of the position of the prudent and crafty steward is that of the anonymous woman who imprudently broke the alabaster flask.

48

The Mystery of the Betrayal

Then Judas Iscariot, who was one of the twelve, went to the chief priests in order to betray him to them. And when they heard it they were glad, and promised to give him money. And he sought an opportunity to betray him.

And on the first day of Unleavened Bread, when they sacrificed the passover lamb, his disciples said to him, "Where will you have us go and prepare for you to eat the passover?" And he sent two of his disciples, and said to them, "Go into the city, and a man carrying a jar of water will meet you; follow him, and wherever he enters, say to the householder, 'The Teacher says, Where is my guest room, where I am to eat the passover with my disciples?' And he will show you a large upper room furnished and ready; there prepare for us." And the disciples set out and went to the city, and found it as he had told them; and they prepared the passover.

And when it was evening he came with the twelve. And as they were at table eating, Jesus said, "Truly, I say to you, one of you will betray me, one who is eating with me." They began to be sorrowful, and to say to him one after another, "Is it I?" He said to them, "It is one of the twelve, one who is dipping bread in the same dish with me. For the Son of man goes as it is written of him, but woe to that man by whom the Son of man is betrayed! It would have been better for that man if he had not been born." (14:10-21)

The betrayal of Christ by one of His own followers has in it an element of mystery. What is hard to understand is not that treachery would appear within the intimate group, for defection is a common human experience. The real difficulty comes in understanding why a specific act of betrayal was necessary. If Christ appeared openly during His entrance into Jerusalem and later in the temple, His bitter enemies would have no trouble in identifying Him. Why, then, would Judas be needed to guide the attackers? If Christ's actions were as open as we might suppose, the chief priests were wasting their money by hiring Judas as a conspirator.

We do not know the full answer to this question, but we get some light upon it when we realize that, even after the entry into Jerusalem, the small group still exhibited some of the characteristics of an underground movement. As in the former case of the finding of the ass, for use in the triumphal entry, so now it appears that secret arrangements had been made. Christ did some things in the public gaze, but He evidently wanted to have the Passover meal to be an undisturbed and therefore a secret occasion. To accomplish this the previous arrangements were fairly elaborate, though of such a nature that they would not be detected by His enemies or by ordinary inhabitants. The man bearing the pitcher of water was part of the underground arrangement, while others who were part of the same system had prepared the room. Perhaps Christ already suspected some treachery within the fellowship of the Twelve and, by this preparatory plan, made sure that the Passover meal itself would not be the occasion of the expected arrest or intrusion by the authorities.

The meal in the secret guest chamber began on a sorrowful note. Christ, by this time, seemed to know that defection was in the air and that the disloyalty was in the inner circle to which He had given so much affectionate attention. Perhaps one of the more loyal disciples, beyond the Twelve, had learned of the treacherous visit of Judas to the chief priests. Perhaps Christ merely sensed that something was wrong. In either case the disappointment was great, chiefly because He had staked everything on the effort to build this little fellowship of inadequate men into something of enduring power. If it started to go to pieces, because of the disloyalty of one, what might occur to the others? Would the fellowship be dissolved, even before the tragic end? This valid question meant that the stakes were high. The Passover meal became the final urgent effort to hold the redemptive fellowship together.

49

Divine Transfusion

And as they were eating, he took bread, and blessed, and broke it, and gave it to them, and said, "Take; this is my body." And he took a cup, and when he had given thanks he gave it to them, and they all drank of it. And he said to them, "This is my blood of the covenant, which is poured out for many. Truly, I say to you, I shall not drink again of the fruit of the vine until that day when I drink it new in the kingdom of God."

And when they had sung a hymn, they went out to the Mount of Olives. And Jesus said to them, "You will all fall away; for it is written, 'I will strike the shepherd, and the sheep will be scattered.' But after I am raised up, I will go before you to Galilee." Peter said to him, "Even though they all fall away, I will not." And Jesus said to him, "Truly, I say to you, this very night, before the cock crows twice, you will deny me three times." But he said vehemently, "If I must die with you, I will not deny you." And they all said the same. (14:22–31)

The Passover meal was a time of surpassing significance to every devout Jew. To the Twelve who gathered with Christ for the last of many meals with Him, the Passover was a vivid reminder of the way in which God had, with a mighty act, saved His people in Egypt when they were unable to save themselves. To those who understood the occasion at all, the experience was one of profound religious feeling. Christ built upon this feeling and gave it a still greater significance, by using the occasion to explain His own impending death and ultimate victory in newness of life.

The meal turned out to be an acted parable. This meant that the meaning was even more clear than that involved in an ordinary spoken parable. By taking bread and breaking the loaf and distributing it, Christ was able to show that the apparent destruction could lead to actual new strength in all who thus shared. The bread that is distributed seems to be lost, but is not. Likewise, Christ taught, the tragedy of His physical destruction would not be permanent, but was the necessary condition of new and risen life, not only in Himself, but in all those who truly shared. The broken bread thus becomes a potent symbol of shared life.

It is the same with drink as with solid food. Unless it is *spent* it cannot be really saved, for it is saved only when it becomes the means of new life and power. This paradox of gain through loss is demonstrated in every common meal of ordinary families, but it took the insight of Christ to make us see the light it sheds upon the whole of human experience. What men and women need is new life and the blood provides an excellent figure, in that life is not possible without an adequate blood supply. We require a divine transfusion, so that as a consequence our lives can be truly spent.

The fellowship of the Twelve was genuine that night. When Christ handed His closest followers the cup, to symbolize the shared life, all, including Judas, drank of it. Did the traitor almost change his plan? They sang a hymn together and went out, undoubtedly with deep affection, but Christ knew, as He said on another occasion, that "most men's love will grow cold" (Matt. 24:12). Accordingly, He predicted that all of them, and not merely one traitor, would fall away. Not only Peter, but all of the Twelve, were vehement in their protestation of enduring loyalty. They did not keep their brave vows, but the fellowship of the bread and wine was not lost. The memory of it came back potently in later days.

It is a great surprise to some contemporary Christians to realize that, so far as the Synoptic Gospels are concerned, we have no indication that Christ commanded the performance of what we call the Eucharist or Holy Communion. "This do in remembrance of me," which appears in some texts of Luke 22:19, does not appear in the best texts. *The Book of Common Prayer*, which asserts that Christ in His Holy Gospel did institute a perpetual memory, is not really accurate. The main dependence has, in fact, been upon the words of the Apostle Paul in I Corinthians 11:23–25. What is important to know is that the earliest gospel represents Christ, not as commanding a ceremony, but as using common food and drink to explain His victory over death and apparent defeat.

50

The Lord's Prayer in Gethsemane

And they went to a place which was called Gethsemane; and he said to his disciples, "Sit here, while I pray." And he took with him Peter and James and John, and began to be greatly distressed and troubled. And he said to them, "My soul is very sorrowful, even to death; remain here, and watch." And going a little farther, he fell on the ground and prayed that, if it were possible, the hour might pass from him. And he said, "Abba, Father, all things are possible to thee; remove this cup from me; yet not what I will, but what thou wilt." And he came and found them sleeping, and he said to Peter, "Simon, are you asleep? Could you not watch one hour? Watch and pray that you may not enter into temptation; the spirit indeed is willing, but the flesh is weak." And again he went away and prayed, saying the same words. And again he came and found them sleeping, for their eyes were very heavy; and they did not know what to answer him. And he came the third time, and said to them, "Are you still sleeping and taking your rest? It is enough; the hour has come; the Son of man is betrayed into the hands of sinners. Rise, let us be going; see, my betrayer is at hand." (14:32–42)

We do not understand fully the sorrow of Christ during the night after the meal with the Twelve, but we can sense something of it. Much of the sorrow evidently had to do with His disappointment. This becomes increasingly clear as we begin to see the way in which Christ depended on the fellowship He was building by His concentration on the task of teaching them in such a manner that they would weather the coming storm. If they should fail, all would fail, because no other way had been provided. These few were the vital link between the earthly life of Christ and the Living Church, which would be in the world as Christ's body after the earthly body was broken.

As on other crucial occasions, Christ, at Gethsemane, took with Him to His place of withdrawal only the Three, Peter, James, and John. Inadequate as they were, He had come to depend more on these fishermen than on any others. But because even this degree of retirement was not sufficient, Christ went on alone, leaving the Three by themselves, and then He prayed in desperate earnestness.

Few events in Christ's life bring Him closer to us than does His prayer at Gethsemane. Every lonely individual who is confronted with some situation in which he does not know where to turn, or in which he faces real defeat, can remember with profit the intensity with which Christ prayed. Christ, in short, seems close to us, in spite of the contrast between His perfection and our failure, because He did not feel self-sufficient. The self-sufficient do not pray.

At the heart of Christ's prayer was the desire to be completely submissive to God's will. Perhaps this is how every prayer, no matter how great the inner turmoil, should end. Christ did not want to fail; He did not want the sacred fellowship to dissolve; but, at the end of His prayer, He was able to envisage anything with equanimity, because as God's Chosen One, He was utterly committed to the Father's will. Even the cup of defeat He could drink, if that should be part of the divine intention.

After finding Peter and the others asleep, and uttering a warning against temptation, Christ found it necessary to withdraw for prayer again. Indeed, the same essential prayer was prayed three times. The quick, the single, the perfunctory prayer could not suffice at Gethsemane. It will not suffice in any crisis.

How did the author of our gospel know the words of Christ's prayer which are included in our text? They could not have been reported by those who overheard, for Christ was alone. The very ones who might have listened were asleep. The only possible conclusion is that Christ took the trouble to tell the members of the inner circle what the essence of His prayer had been. If He took the trouble to do this, as must have been the case, it was His way of indicating how important, for the Christian, the prayer of divine acceptance really is. It was, indeed, the Lord's Prayer.

51

The Arrest

And immediately, while he was still speaking, Judas
came, one of the twelve, and with him a crowd with
swords and clubs, from the chief priests and the scribes
and the elders. Now the betrayer had given them a sign,
saying, "The one I shall kiss is the man; seize him and
lead him away safely." And when he came, he went up
to him at once, and said, "Master!" And he kissed him.
And they laid hands on him and seized him. But one of
those who stood by drew his sword, and struck the slave
of the high priest and cut off his ear. And Jesus said to
them, "Have you come out as against a robber, with
swords and clubs to capture me? Day after day I was
with you in the temple teaching, and you did not seize
me. But let the scriptures be fulfilled." And they all for-
sook him, and fled.

And a young man followed him, with nothing but a
linen cloth about his body; and they seized him, but he
left the linen cloth and ran away naked. (14:43–52)

Since only the Three had gone forward with Christ
close to His place of prayer in the Garden, Judas, having
stayed behind with the others, was free to make his
contact with the police. The fact that they came at night,

using Judas as a guide, indicates that, in their thought at least, the Christian movement was seen as both subversive and secret. A member of the cell was helping them to apprehend the Leader of the cell.

The police must have expected resistance, for they arrived in considerable force and were well armed. Being unfamiliar with the Galilean visitors to the city, they had arranged for Judas to indicate, by a kiss, which one the Leader was. The agreed sign was a natural one to indicate the relationship of pupil and teacher. It is important to realize, not only that Christ did not resist, but also that the only one who failed to follow His example was an anonymous spectator. This evidence of self-control on the part of Christ's followers is really impressive.

If we are perplexed at the necessity of paying Judas to perform the act of betrayal, we are in good company, for Christ expressed His own perplexity. Why, He asked, did they need to come physically armed, as though He were a bandit in hiding? He reminded them that He had been openly in the temple each day since arrival in the city and that, consequently, they could have apprehended Him at any time they might have chosen. So far as we know, He received no answer, so that the betrayal is still, in part, a mystery.

Our best clue to the usefulness of Judas is the idea that, by employing him, the religious authorities were preparing their case against Christ in such a way as to incriminate Him in the eyes of the Romans and thus insure His execution. They could not make an impressive case by arresting one who was engaged in open religious teaching, especially when that teaching was clearly appealing to the rank and file of the people. The Roman authorities persistently refused to meddle in what they considered purely religious matters and in this sense they upheld religious freedom. It was only when civil power was in jeopardy that they were concerned. By using Judas, therefore, and by treating Jesus as a revolutionary leader who had to be taken both by force and by stealth, the image of the subversive movement was made presentable. The Romans would not condemn a mere teacher, but they would not have any mercy on one who claimed to be King of the Jews.

The identity of the young man who fled naked, leaving his linen cloth behind him, is not known. Many have guessed that the young man was John Mark and that this tiny reference is really his signature to the earliest gospel narrative. It must be remembered, however, that this is pure speculation. Neither Matthew nor Luke thought the incident of sufficient importance to reproduce it. The only point of real significance is that the story serves to emphasize the near universality of the panic which was exhibited by Christ's trusted followers. The sad element of the story is the fact that the continuing loyalty of one brave person was *news*. The Apostles, after all their protestations of faithfulness, ran away in the beginning.

52

The Ecclesiastical Court

And they led Jesus to the high priest; and all the chief priests and the elders and the scribes were assembled. And Peter had followed him at a distance, right into the courtyard of the high priest; and he was sitting with the guards, and warming himself at the fire. Now the chief priests and the whole council sought testimony against Jesus to put him to death; but they found none. For many bore false witness against him, and their witness did not agree. And some stood up and bore false witness against him, saying, "We heard him say, 'I will destroy this temple that is made with hands, and in three days I will build another, not made with hands.'" Yet not even so did their testimony agree. And the high priest stood up in the midst, and asked Jesus, "Have you no answer to make? What is it that these men testify against you?" But he was silent and made no answer. Again the high priest asked him, "Are you the Christ, the Son of the Blessed?" And Jesus said, "I am; and you will see the Son of man sitting at the right hand of Power, and coming with the clouds of heaven." And the high priest tore his mantle, and said, "Why do we still need witnesses? You have heard his blasphemy. What is your decision?" And they all condemned him as deserving death. And some began to spit on him, and to cover his face, and to strike him, saying to him, "Prophesy!" And the guards received him with blows. (14:53–65)

The night of the Passover was filled with memorable events. It included the undisturbed meal, the Gethsemane retreat, the arrest by the police, and the trial before the Sanhedrin. All of this went on before morning. The trial was really a preliminary investigation, an effort to discover a charge on the basis of which Jesus might be handed over to Pilate. The religious leaders desired Christ's death, but they hoped to place the responsibility for the death sentence upon the Roman Procurator.

The task before the Sanhedrin was not an easy one. How could they find any valid grounds of condemnation in one who healed the sick, who fed the multitude, and who was obviously kind as well as brave? Perhaps they hoped that He would resist arrest and thus be marked as a disturber of the peace, but, if that was the intention, they were disappointed. How can judgment be passed on one who teaches the love of God and the love of one's neighbor? Dependable and damaging witnesses were hard to find, even though several were called.

When the charge was made that Jesus had threatened the destruction of the temple, He made no reply whatever. Why reply to willful and perverse misunderstanding? He had indeed said that the temple, being made of physical materials, was not permanent, and He had referred to the temple of His own body and its resurrection, but people who thought this was blasphemous would not understand any further explanation. Christ did not waste His words; He did not cast pearls before swine.

The second line of attack was far more important and was the one which led ultimately to Christ's official condemnation. When the high priest posed the direct question, whether Jesus was the expected Messiah, he received a direct and unequivocal answer. Christ said simply that He was the Messiah and that, furthermore, they would see His ultimate triumph. Jesus died for claiming to be King of the Jews.

To claim to be the Messiah was not blasphemy, though the high priest said that it was, but it was obviously the one charge that could be passed on, impressively, to the Roman court. The fact that Jesus had reinterpreted the concept of the Messiah, rejecting the image of the military or civil leader, and interpreting His role as that of the suffering servant, did not save Him from the jealous Roman power. If He claimed to be King, even though He altered completely the popular idea of what kingship meant, that was sufficient for the imperial mind. The Sanhedrin had found what it sought.

53

The Flaw in the Rock

And as Peter was below in the courtyard, one of the maids of the high priest came; and seeing Peter warming himself, she looked at him, and said, "You also were with the Nazarene, Jesus." But he denied it, saying, "I neither know nor understand what you mean." And he went out into the gateway. And the maid saw him, and began again to say to the bystanders, "This man is one of them." But again he denied it. And after a little while again the bystanders said to Peter, "Certainly you are one of them; for you are a Galilean." But he began to invoke a curse on himself and to swear, "I do not know this man of whom you speak." And immediately the cock crowed a second time. And Peter remembered how Jesus had said to him, "Before the cock crows twice, you will deny me three times." And he broke down and wept. (14:66–72)

The shameful story of Peter's denial of Christ must have come from Peter's own lips. If, as Papias said, the earliest gospel was written by Mark, who took down what Peter said, we have, in part, a record of early Christian preaching. In that case it is clear that Peter did not spare himself. He had something to be ashamed of and he told it openly.

The situation of Peter in the courtyard of the high priest was one of essential paradox. He could neither stay away nor could he make a courageous witness, with all of its attendant risks. Peter was drawn to Christ, but, as he must have told many times later, and as Mark may have noted at the time, he was not drawn closely enough to be willing to die with Him.

The character of Peter is endlessly fascinating. There was a sense in which he was the leader of the Twelve, always a part of the innermost circle. In any case it was he who first recognized the tremendous fact that Jesus was the expected Messiah. On one side of his character, he was bold and imaginative, while on the other he was weak and vacillating. It was, said Christ, on this poor kind of rock, or rubble, that He would be able to build His church. Thus this weak and lovable and changeable man was nicknamed "The Rock," apparently with essential humor. The pathos of the nickname was demonstrated in the courtyard of the Sanhedrin, when this supposedly firm man could not even bear to admit to one of the maids that he had been Christ's companion.

What is important to remember is that Peter's cowardice was not the end of the story. Weak and vacillating as he was, this man became, after Christ's earthly story was finished, a veritable bulwark of the new faith. The story is helpful because it shows how Christ can use inadequate men.

The claim that Peter was the first Pope has nothing in the New Testament to substantiate it. Popes, indeed, finally came to be appointed in Rome, but there were no such officials among the first generation of Christians. Peter was in no way separated from common life and its problems. He was married; he had a mother-in-law; he was extremely fallible; he sinned and repented exactly as other men must do. It is not probable that Christ, having to fight the religious hierarchy at all points, would establish one of His own. It would have been relatively easy for Him to set up a religious establishment of His own, with some men in authority over others, but His conception was too revolutionary for that. What He attempted to do, instead, was to build up an intense fellowship of humble men in the conviction that such a fellowship could be truly redemptive. We are always tempted to read back into the gospel story our own prejudices and assumptions based on later practice, but the realism of the gospel story is a constant check on this tendency. Nowhere is the check more needed than in regard to Peter.

54

Pilate before Christ

And as soon as it was morning the chief priests, with the elders and scribes, and the whole council held a consultation; and they bound Jesus and led him away and delivered him to Pilate. And Pilate asked him, "Are you the King of the Jews?" And he answered him, "You have said so." And the chief priests accused him of many things. And Pilate again asked him, "Have you no answer to make? See how many charges they bring against you." But Jesus made no further answer, so that Pilate wondered.

Now at the feast he used to release for them any one prisoner whom they asked. And among the rebels in prison, who had committed murder in the insurrection, there was a man called Barabbas. And the crowd came up and began to ask Pilate to do as he was wont to do for them. And he answered them, "Do you want me to release for you the King of the Jews?" For he perceived that it was out of envy that the chief priests had delivered him up. But the chief priests stirred up the crowd to have him release for them Barabbas instead. And Pilate again said to them, "Then what shall I do with the man whom you call the King of the Jews?" And they cried out again, "Crucify him." And Pilate said to them, "Why, what evil has he done?" But they shouted all the more, "Crucify him." So Pilate, wishing to satisfy the crowd, released for them Barabbas; and having scourged Jesus, he delivered him to be crucified. (15:1–15)

A proud and brutal Roman, Pontius Pilate, was Procurator of Judea A.D. 26–36. Though of only equestrian rank, and therefore in general subordinate to the Governor of Syria, Pilate, by the coincidence of Christ's death, is better known today than almost any other Roman of his period. He had a deep contempt for the people he ruled; he crushed riots mercilessly and continually ordered executions. The religious leaders, in handing Christ over to this vicious man, had a good chance of success in their effort to destroy the Christian movement by insuring the death of its Leader.

Little could the proud Roman know that his confrontation with the accused Leader was the most important event of his life. What is almost sure to strike us as surprising in Mark's account of the trial is Pilate's evident judgment that the incident was essentially trivial. He was, indeed, surprised that Christ did not bother to answer the accusations of the priests and that, furthermore, He did not answer the Procurator when he mentioned it. But Pilate did not press the matter and soon turned to the practical question of deciding which malefactor to set free. He teased the religious authorities a little about releasing Jesus, but then, when the pressure was great, gave in to the mob and released Barabbas instead. He then had Jesus scourged and sent Him to be crucified. For the Roman, this was all in the day's work, just part of the necessary task of keeping a troublesome society in order. The probability is that he never thought of the affair again, except briefly when Joseph of Arimathea went to him to ask for the corpse. Even then, all was businesslike, with no evidence of remorse.

The trial was, of course, far more a trial of the Roman than it was of the Galilean. The most damaging revelation it made of Pilate's character was not of his ruthless cruelty, but of his almost playful mood. There is no evidence that scourging and death by crucifixion moved him at all. Though he recognized the innocence of Jesus and the political harmlessness of His movement, Pilate kept himself uninvolved. He could see the scheming of the religious leaders, but this was not a matter of sufficient importance to require of him a courageous stand. Even the accusation against Jesus, that He claimed to be King of the Jews, was, to Pilate, something slightly amusing. His condemnation is that he was not sensitive enough to have any idea of who Christ was.

It is no exoneration of Pilate to say that the Roman official had no understanding of what he was doing. The fact that he did not understand was his essential condemnation, for it revealed his character. Pilate illustrated admirably the truth of Christ's words, "By what judgment you judge you will be judged."

55

Passage to Golgotha

And the soldiers led him away inside the palace (that is, the praetorium); and they called together the whole battalion. And they clothed him in a purple cloak, and plaiting a crown of thorns they put it on him. And they began to salute him, "Hail, King of the Jews!" And they struck his head with a reed, and spat upon him, and they knelt down in homage to him. And when they had mocked him, they stripped him of the purple cloak, and put his own clothes on him. And they led him out to crucify him.

And they compelled a passer-by, Simon of Cyrene, who was coming in from the country, the father of Alexander and Rufus, to carry his cross. And they brought him to the place called Golgotha (which means the place of a skull). And they offered him wine mingled with myrrh; but he did not take it. (15:16–23)

The mood of lightheartedness in the presence of tragic sorrow seems to have been passed on from Pilate to the soldiers who led Christ away to the place of execution. This matter about His being a King was, it seemed to them, an excellent joke, so they put on a farcical act of obeisance to Him. It was clearly the accusation against

Jesus which prompted the mockery, the mockery being one evidence of how well known the accusation was.

In many ways the mockery must have been harder for Christ to endure than the bitter hatred of the Sanhedrin. Ridicule is always a deeply wounding weapon. The contrast between this lone figure, who somehow claimed to be King, and Caesar, who wore an actual crown, was so great that these soldiers of Caesar were much amused. They decided to give Jesus a crown, like Caesar's except that, in derision, they made it of thorns. In a deep sense the crucifixion had already begun.

After the little play, mingled with cruelty and mock obeisance, was over, the men led Christ out for the actual execution. Though it was customary for the criminal to carry his own cross bar, on which he would be crucified, Christ seems to have been so weakened by the cruel treatment already received that He was not strong enough to carry it. Accordingly, a passer-by was drafted for this ignominious task. There is no reason to suppose that this drafted man, Simon of Cyrene, had ever seen Jesus before, but the brief experience apparently moved him so deeply that it drew both him and his children into the Christian movement. No disciple was attracted to Christ under more sorrowful circumstances. The fact that Simon could thus be moved by Christ's response to cruelty tells us a great deal about how Christ bore Himself on the way to Golgotha.

The children of Simon, Alexander and Rufus, were so well known to Mark's readers that the writer did not need to explain them more fully. It is possible that Rufus is the one mentioned in Romans 16:13, but this we do not know. All that we really know is that even Christ's walk to the cross was an occasion for evangelizing.

Just before the final act of execution, Christ was offered a drink which was drugged, but He refused to take it. He met His death, not in a semistupor, but with all his senses intact. His pain was not dulled by a soporific.

In a society like ours in which anaesthetics are taken for granted, it is hard for us to realize how terrible raw, undulled pain can be. We sometimes forget that such was the lot, at one time or another, of nearly every one of our remote ancestors. We are glad, and we ought to be glad, that effective anaesthetics have been invented, for they remove from human life some of its worst forms of misery, but, at the same time, we can be glad that Christ neither sought nor accepted help at this point. The result is that everyone who is enduring severe pain of any kind is entitled to remember that the Lord, Himself, endured pain also. We do not know, in any adequate sense, the answer to the problem of evil, and specifically we do not know why God permitted so much pain in His created world, but we know that His own Beloved Son shared it.

56

Silence on the Cross

And they crucified him, and divided his garments among them, casting lots for them, to decide what each should take. And it was the third hour, when they crucified him. And the inscription of the charge against him read, "The King of the Jews." And with him they crucified two robbers, one on his right and one on his left. And those who passed by derided him, wagging their heads, and saying, "Aha! You who would destroy the temple and build it in three days, save yourself, and come down from the cross!" So also the chief priests mocked him to one another with the scribes, saying, "He saved others; he cannot save himself. Let the Christ, the King of Israel, come down now from the cross, that we may see and believe." Those who were crucified with him also reviled him. (15:24–32)

The cruelty of men is potentially so great that it can hardly be exaggerated. There are few scenes in which mankind demonstrates its unloveliness more than in a mob. The members of the mob are wonderfully safe, for the victim is wholly at their mercy. They know that they are invulnerable because the lone person is not in a position to defend himself. This is why mob action is essentially cowardly. It is cowardly because the many who bait the one run no personal risks. Mob action is, accordingly, among the most despicable of human actions.

Christ's treatment at the crucifixion demonstrated what is most evil in mob behavior. Instead of being moved to compassion by Christ's physical torment, as the weight of His body pulled against the open wounds of the nails, the people who came to watch the spectacle rejoiced in His agony and ridiculed Him. The chief point of ridicule was the contrast between His former claims and the eventual outcome. Many supposed that what they observed was a fall which came after overweening pride. He claimed, they mistakenly thought, to be able to destroy and rebuild the temple and here He could not even save His own physical body. What had become, they wanted to know, of His great pretensions? If He could do such great things, why could he not work a miracle and come away from the cross, unharmed?

The accusation, which was written out and attached to the cross, shows how deeply the question of royal claims had entered into public mentality. Both this and the railings of the spectators reproduced the fundamental charge against Him, as indicated by the first question which Pilate asked Him.

The loneliness of Christ on the cross must have been almost unbearable. Where were the disciples? Where were the Twelve, to whom He had given so much? Where were the many who had been healed and fed? All of the present group were against Him, including even the men who were executed with Him. We have to read Luke's account to learn that one of them finally changed and became a disciple before he died. We might have expected the religious leaders to maintain a dignified absence from the scene, but they came to gloat over their triumph, forgetful of their dignity. Perhaps they thought they would make Him answer them, but, if this was the purpose, they did not succeed. He bore all of their mocking in silence. If they had not understood earlier, it was not likely that they would understand in their time of apparent triumph.

We have made much, in Good Friday observances, of Christ's words on the cross, but we might note, even more, His silences on the cross. What is really amazing, in the record, is the inference that He was silent for six full hours, from the third to the ninth. The time when we should most expect Him to cry out in anguish, the time of the actual nailing, was marked by complete silence, so far as our record tells us. We are grateful to Mark for letting us know how long the silent period was. This the other authors neglected to say.

57

Death of Christ

And when the sixth hour had come, there was darkness over the whole land until the ninth hour. And at the ninth hour Jesus cried with a loud voice, "Elo-i, Elo-i, lama sabachthani?" which means, "My God, my God, why hast thou forsaken me?" And some of the bystanders hearing it said, "Behold, he is calling Elijah." And one ran and, filling a sponge full of vinegar, put it on a reed and gave it to him to drink, saying, "Wait, let us see whether Elijah will come to take him down." And Jesus uttered a loud cry, and breathed his last. And the curtain of the temple was torn in two, from top to bottom. And when the centurion, who stood facing him, saw that he thus breathed his last, he said, "Truly this man was a son of God!"

There were also women looking on from afar, among whom were Mary Magdalene, and Mary the mother of James the younger and of Joses, and Salome, who, when he was in Galilee, followed him, and ministered to him; and also many other women who came up with him to Jerusalem. (15:33–41)

In our system of numeration, the period of agony was from nine o'clock in the morning until three o'clock in the afternoon. At this time, we are told, Christ finally broke the long silence of the cross, by repeating the words from Psalm 22. According to Mark, it was His last clear utterance before death. It was a piercing cry, filling us, even now, with a sense of genuine wonderment. Why, out of all the sacred literature of which His mind was full, did He choose, in His agony, this poignant verse, "My God, my God, why hast thou forsaken me?" Did this, better than any other, express what He felt? Why did He not quote Deuteronomy or one of the Prophets, as on other occasions? All that we know is that He turned to the Psalms, which provide the clearest record of deep religious experience.

Did the use of Psalm 22 indicate that Christ suddenly doubted the entire undertaking? Did it mean that the closeness of the relationship with the Father was at last dubious? What a paradox, if, at the very moment which, to subsequent thought, His closeness to the Father was most evident, He temporarily ceased to feel the reality of the divine relationship! We do not know and we cannot know exactly what was in Christ's mind as He uttered this cry, but we can say that His behavior on the cross convinces us, more than does anything else, that God was in Christ, reconciling the world unto Himself. At the same time it is important to say that every humble person who, in the midst of defeat and temptation, has periods of real doubt, may be strengthened by the realization that even Christ had such a moment. What He said on the cross, far from separating Him from us, brings Him closer to us.

The reason why Christ's expression of perplexity brings

170

Him closer to us is that all of us, if we truly understand our position, are perpetually perplexed. Christianity is not for the overconfident people, just as it is not for the people who suppose that they are righteous. Christianity is based, not on some simple or obvious truism, which no one can doubt, but upon a great faith shadowed by a great fear. We *could* be wrong. The skeptic could be right. Evil and confusion are real and pervasive. The Christian, if he is honest, faces negative as well as positive evidence.

Though most of the observers of Christ's death were callously unmoved and apparently mocking to the end, this was not true of all. The chief priests, claiming to be very religious, were not touched even with compassion, but the Roman military officer became convinced that Christ was what He said He was, the Son of God. Thus the death itself, like the walk to Golgotha, became a means of evangelizing. The only Christians who showed courageous loyalty were a few women. The fact that their courage surpassed that of the male disciples is revealing. James and John were not there, but their mother was. From that day to this the place of women in the Christian cause has been tremendous.

58

Burial of Christ

And when evening had come, since it was the day of Preparation, that is, the day before the sabbath, Joseph of Arimathea, a respected member of the council, who was also himself looking for the kingdom of God, took courage and went to Pilate, and asked for the body of Jesus. And Pilate wondered if he were already dead; and summoning the centurion, he asked him whether he was already dead. And when he learned from the centurion that he was dead, he granted the body to Joseph. And he bought a linen shroud, and taking him down, wrapped him in the linen shroud, and laid him in a tomb which had been hewn out of the rock; and he rolled a stone against the door of the tomb. Mary Magdalene and Mary the mother of Joses saw where he was laid. (15:42–47)

The crucifixion took place on the day before the Sabbath, that is, on Friday. Because the Sabbath began at sundown, and also because dead criminals had to be buried before nightfall, speed was required in disposing of Christ's body. It was necessary to receive the permission of the Procurator, in order to take possession of the body, but one man, Joseph of Arimathea, had both the courage and the standing to be able to make the official request. Pilate was not willing to grant permission for burial until he had checked with the centurion, to make sure that Jesus had really died. Did the centurion, in addition to the bare item of information, tell Pilate of his conclusion that the One they had killed was more than man? This we do not know, nor do we know of his subsequent career, but we may reasonably look on this Roman officer as one of the first of the long line of Gentile Christians.

We wish we could know, likewise, of the subsequent service of Joseph of Arimathea, but in any case we recognize, with gratitude, the courageous part he played in the act of burial. After others had taken pains to be detached from the events, Joseph made his own involvement unambiguous. In order to stay within the time limit, he hastily placed Christ's body in a rock tomb, of the kind then much used. The purchase of fine linen in which to wrap Christ's body was a way of showing genuine respect. This man's deed thus stands in sharp contrast to that of most of the others who had any contact with Christ that day. Joseph certainly ran great risk by providing a tomb as well as burial service. If the public attack, which had been centered on Christ, were to be extended to His followers, this distinguished man would naturally be singled out for special treatment. In short, his willingness to care for the body of the One whom he loved, when others paid no attention or retreated in safety, was a bold witness to his faith.

After the burial in the hewn rock, a large stone was placed before the opening, presumably to keep out animals or thieves. It appears that the Twelve, in contrast to all their protestations of faithfulness, not only stayed away from the execution, but even from the burial. Again, it was a few women, specifically the two named Mary, who were faithful and brave. These two women were spectators of the burial, so that they could easily remember the exact location.

It is probable that the Christian account of the crucifixion, as well as of the burial of Christ, goes back, ultimately, to the testimony of a few faithful women. Mark makes no suggestion, however, that the mother of Jesus was one of the witnesses. One of the most interesting references is that to Mary of Magdala, who all the gospels agree was present at the crucifixion and, according to Mark, at both the burial and resurrection. Actually her part in the development of Christ's cause was immense. If there had been feminine apostles, she would undoubtedly have been one. We learn from Luke, for instance, that she was one of the women who, in Galilee, moved along with Christ and His other followers, contributing to the support of the movement. She had reason to be grateful for she is described as one from whom seven devils had been driven out. She may be considered as the leading feminine disciple.

59

Resurrection of Christ

And when the sabbath was past, Mary Magdalene, Mary the mother of James, and Salome bought spices, so that they might go and anoint him. And very early on the first day of the week they went to the tomb when the sun had risen. And they were saying to one another, "Who will roll away the stone for us from the door of the tomb?" And looking up, they saw that the stone was rolled back; for it was very large. And entering the tomb, they saw a young man sitting on the right side, dressed in a white robe; and they were amazed. And he said to them, "Do not be amazed; you seek Jesus of Nazareth, who was crucified. He has risen, he is not here; see the place where they laid him. But go, tell his disciples and Peter that he is going before you to Galilee; there you will see him, as he told you." And they went out and fled from the tomb; for trembling and astonishment had come upon them; and they said nothing to any one, for they were afraid. (16:1–8)

The part played by women becomes increasingly greater as the gospel narrative comes to an end. After the cessation of activity, which the Sabbath necessitated, that is, on what we call Sunday morning, three of the inner circle of women attempted to do what they were not allowed to do earlier, anoint Christ's body. Clearly, they wished, out of love and respect for their lost Master, to provide a service somewhat comparable to that of embalming. But, the gospel tells us, they never achieved this purpose for they encountered a great surprise. They found the tomb empty, with the closing stone rolled away.

The amazement of the women was increased, rather than diminished by the message which a young wan, who was sitting in the tomb, delivered to them. The message of the angelic visitor was that Christ was risen from the dead. That the angel's great concern was for the little group is exactly what we should expect when we realize the degree to which the success of the entire movement depended on the continuing vitality of the Apostolic fellowship. Accordingly the women were commissioned to find Christ's intimate followers and to give them the news that they could join their Master in Galilee, where He had first called them. In this commission, the name of Peter, as a recipient of the news, is dissociated from the others, perhaps because of his disgraceful defection in the courtyard of the high priest.

The indication is that Christ had to rise from the dead in order to keep the potentially redemptive fellowship from complete decay and dissolution. In any case we know that the fellowship was already disintegrating and that the men, whose hopes had been so high only a few days earlier, were going back home in utter discouragement. We also know that, not long afterward, the fellowship was renewed and the faith so deepened that it lasted through all the lives of these men, in spite of the persecution which was practically continuous and universal.

There are people, even among those who like to call themselves Christians, who refuse to believe in the physical resurrection of Jesus Christ. The miracle seems to them too great to be believed. We must honor such people for their effort to be intellectually honest, but it is relevant to point out that they, in their unbelief, face an essentially insoluble problem. How can they account for the complete and lasting change in the lives of the Apostles? What event, apart from the actual and literal resurrection, could be stupendous enough to change these humble persons from defeated men to men who were bold as lions, not temporarily, but for all of the rest of their days? It is easy to talk about wishful thinking and delusion, but such hypotheses do not really account for known facts. In any case the men themselves, though dubious at first, became utterly convinced that Christ had risen. There is no doubt that the affirmation of the resurrection as a fact became the central substance of Apostolic preaching, even when it was met by ridicule. "If Christ has not been raised," said Paul, "then our preaching is in vain" (I Cor. 15:14). There is no doubt that the chapter on the resurrection is the climax of the entire story.

60

The Eternal Christ

Now when he rose early on the first day of the week, he appeared first to Mary Magdalene, from whom he had cast out seven demons. She went and told those who had been with him, as they mourned and wept. But when they heard that he was alive and had been seen by her, they would not believe it.

After this he appeared in another form to two of them, as they were walking into the country. And they went back and told the rest, but they did not believe them.

Afterward he appeared to the eleven themselves as they sat at table; and he upbraided them for their unbelief and hardness of heart, because they had not believed those who saw him after he had risen. And he said to them, "Go into all the world and preach the gospel to the whole creation. He who believes and is baptized will be saved; but he who does not believe will be condemned. And these signs will accompany those who believe: in my name they will cast out demons; they will speak in new tongues; they will pick up serpents, and if they drink any deadly thing, it will not hurt them; they will lay their hands on the sick; and they will recover."

So then the Lord Jesus, after he had spoken to them, was taken up into heaven, and sat down at the right hand of God. And they went forth and preached everywhere, while the Lord worked with them and confirmed the message by the signs that attended it. Amen. (16:9–20)

In some ancient manuscripts of Mark's gospel there are two alternative endings to the narrative. The longer of these endings, which appears as 16:9–20, is not printed in the regular text of some modern versions, because in style and vocabulary it is distinct from the rest of the gospel. In this case the book ends with verse 8, though this is not satisfactory, because the narrative breaks off there so suddenly. Even though the longer ending is disputed, there is value in being acquainted with it because there is much in it which is helpful to those who seek to confront Jesus Christ to the end.

Again we find the importance of the women witnesses, who were the very first to whom Christ appeared. The risen Christ is pictured as coming to His followers in small groups, rather than in some public spectacle. In all cases, there is deep doubt, involving genuine resistance to the story which the happy women told. The really convincing appearance came to the residue of the Twelve when they were all together again, perhaps for the first time after the Passover meal with the subsequent defection and death of Judas. Undoubtedly Christ appeared to the Apostles as they ate together, both because this was a reminder of the last supper and because it was the fellowship that was precious. From the beginning the major followers had been more than lone and separated individuals. Henceforth their sacred fellowship, with the

Eternal Christ as their seen or unseen Guest, was the creative center of their lives.

As Christ had earlier, in a crucial decision, sent His followers out two by two, so now, in a still larger step, He made their ministry universal. He told them to go "into all the world." Too often, we have understood these great words in a merely geographical or extensive sense. It is equally reasonable to understand them in an intensive sense. Christ's ambassadors, then, are required to go *into* politics, *into* business, *into* homes, *into* education. The purpose of the gospel is to penetrate the whole of common life, making confrontation with Christ a universal and potentially redemptive experience. A fitting conclusion is found in the words of a shorter alternative ending: "And after this Jesus himself sent out by means of them, from east to west, the sacred and imperishable proclamation of eternal salvation."

Almighty and most merciful Father, who has sent thy Son Jesus Christ into the world to redeem the world, grant that this commemoration of His life and passion may quicken my repentance, increase my hope, strengthen my faith, and enlarge my charity. Amen.